W0286276

Langenscheidt

Englisch

Telefonieren leicht gemacht

Für Beruf und Alltag

Von Lynn Weston

Langenscheidt

Berlin · München · Wien · Zürich · New York

Verwendete Symbole

= Vertonter Text auf Audio-CD

= Tipps und Informationen zur Telekommunikation

= Siehe

Umwelthinweis: gedruckt auf chlorfrei gebleichtem Papier

Umschlaggestaltung: Independent Medien-Design

© 1998, 2001 Langenscheidt KG, Berlin und München
Druck: Druckhaus Langenscheidt, Berlin
Printed in Germany
ISBN 3-468-29934-6
www.langenscheidt.de

2. 3. 4. 5. 6. * 07 06 05 04 03

Inhalt

Vorwort

»Englisch telefonieren leicht gemacht« ist ideal für alle, die regelmäßig auf Englisch telefonieren. Dieses Buch ist als Selbstlernkurs konzipiert und bietet Anfängern mit Vorkenntnissen und Fortgeschrittenen das sprachliche Know-how für berufliche und private Telefongespräche.

Die zehn Einheiten bzw. Musterdialoge bauen von der Planung und Ausführung bis zum Abschluss eines Projektes thematisch aufeinander auf; sie bieten ein abgerundetes Bild der Geschäfts- und Berufswelt. Im Zentrum steht jeweils ein Telefondialog zum Hören und Nachsprechen sowie zum Üben (Dialogpraxis).

Jede Einheit enthält eine Wortschatzauswahl aus der Welt der Telekommunikation.

Die Grammatikübungen und die Kurzgrammatik im Anhang vertiefen Grammatikaspekte, die im alltäglichen Gespräch gebraucht werden.

Eine Schreib- bzw. Hörübung (jeweils Übung 3) pro Einheit gibt dem Lerner die Gelegenheit, eine Notiz oder ein Memo zu verfassen – eine Situation wie sie beim Telefonieren häufig auftritt. Die Musterantworten dazu sind jeweils vertont. Ein kurzer Test am Schluss jeder Einheit dient der Vertiefung des Gelernten. Einen Schlüssel zu den Übungen finden Sie im Anhang ab Seite 122.

Die Telefontipps bieten nützliche und praktische Informationen rund um die Welt der Telekommunikation sowie psychologische Einblicke in die Welt des Telefonierens; sie sind größtenteils vertont und vertiefen das Hörverständnis.

Hören bzw. lesen Sie die Musterdialoge am besten mehrmals, bevor Sie mit den Hör- und Sprechübungen bzw. schriftlichen Ergänzungsübungen der »Dialogpraxis« beginnen. Hören und Sprechen sind die wichtigsten Grundkenntnisse, die hier geübt werden. Aus diesem Grund sind die Moderation bzw. die Anleitungen auf der Audio-CD durchgängig auf Englisch gesprochen. Die deutsche Entsprechung dazu finden Sie jeweils im Buch.

Die Übungsform »Dialogpraxis« ist sowohl mündlich mittels der Begleit-CD als auch schriftlich in Form von Einsetzübungen (jeweils A und B) möglich.

Zur Handhabung der Audio-CD bei der Übungsform »Dialogpraxis«:

Die Dialogpraxis dient der Vertiefung des Musterdialogs. Der Übungsdialog ist deshalb langsamer gesprochen als der Musterdialog und mit kurzen Pausen zwischen den einzelnen Sprecherparts versehen.

Die Dialogpraxis auf der CD beinhaltet folgende Übungsformen:

- Hören und Nachsprechen:
  Hören Sie sich den Übungsdialog Absatz für Absatz an, drücken Sie dann die Pausentaste und sprechen Sie den jeweiligen Absatz nach; lassen Sie die Pausentaste wieder los und fahren Sie in der gleichen Weise bis zum Ende fort.
- Übernehmen Sie nacheinander die Rolle des Sprechers A und B:
  Spulen Sie den Übungsdialog auf die Anfangsposition zurück und hören Sie sich nur jeweils die Rolle des Gegenparts an, während Sie die ausgeblendete bzw. überspielte Sprecherrolle selbst übernehmen. Wenn Sie zum Beispiel die Sprecherrolle A ergänzen, dann drücken Sie jeweils nach Äußerungen der Sprecherrolle B auf die Pausentaste, sprechen selbstständig den Dialogteil des Sprechers A, lassen die Pausentaste los und überprüfen, ob Ihre Äußerung korrekt war. Spulen Sie den Übungsdialog dann wieder zurück und übernehmen Sie in gleicher Weise die Sprecherrolle B.

Wichtige Grundbegriffe

Abbreviations/Abkürzungen

e.g.	=	for example	kg	=	kilogramme(s) / kilo(s)
i.e.	=	that is	UK	=	United Kingdom
etc.	=	et cetera	US	=	United States of America
cm	=	centimetre(s)	sb.	=	somebody
km	=	kilometre(s)	sth.	=	something
g	=	gramme(s)			

Days of the Week/Wochentage

Monday	Montag	Friday	Freitag
Tuesday	Dienstag	Saturday	Samstag
Wednesday	Mittwoch	Sunday	Sonntag
Thursday	Donnerstag		

Months/Monate

January	Januar	July	Juli
February	Februar	August	August
March	März	September	September
April	April	October	Oktober
May	Mai	November	November
June	Juni	December	Dezember

Weights and Measures/Maße und Gewichte

1 inch	=	2.54 cm	1 tonne	=	1000 kg
1 foot	=	30.48 cm	1 pint	=	0.56 litres
1 mile	=	1.609 km	1 gallon (UK)	=	4.54 litres
1 ounce	=	28.4 g	1 gallon (US)	=	3.78 litres
1 pound	=	454 g			

Numerals/Grundzahlen

1	one	11	eleven	21	twenty-one
2	two	12	twelve	22	twenty-two
3	three	13	thirteen	23	twenty-three, etc.
4	four	14	fourteen	30	thirty
5	five	15	fifteen	40	forty
6	six	16	sixteen	50	fifty
7	seven	17	seventeen	60	sixty
8	eight	18	eighteen	70	seventy
9	nine	19	nineteen	80	eighty
10	ten	20	twenty	90	ninety

100	a / one hundred
147	a / one hundred and forty-seven
782	seven hundred and eighty-two
1,000	a / one thousand
5,953	five thousand, nine hundred and fifty-three
20,000	twenty thousand
1,000,000	a / one million
6,531,875	six million, five hundred and thirty-one thousand, eight hundred and seventy-five

Money/Geld

UK
100 pence ("p") = 1 pound ("£")
(£10 = "ten pounds")

US
100 cents ("c") = 1 dollar ("$")

Time/Uhrzeit (→ Unit 5 und → Unit 8)

Im Englischen gibt es verschiedene Möglichkeiten, die Uhrzeit auszudrücken. Bei vollen Stunden wird meist der Ausdruck *o'clock* verwendet (Abkürzung für "of the clock" = der Uhr) (z. B. ten o'clock/one o'clock etc.). Bei den »nicht vollen« Stundenangaben entfällt *o'clock* (z. B. ten-thirty = 11.30 h; half past two = 14.30 h).

1 Benutzen Sie Wörter und Wortgruppen, um die Tageszeit, d. h. Vormittag, Nachmittag, Abend oder Nacht, zu spezifizieren. Die 12-Stunden-Uhr wird angewendet (z. B. It's twenty-five past eight in the morning / It's quarter to four in the afternoon).

2 Benutzen Sie die Abkürzungen *a.m.* (= ante meridiem; Vormittag) und *p.m.* (= post meridiem; Nachmittag; Abend), um die Tageszeit zu spezifizieren. Die 12-Stunden-Uhr wird angewendet (z. B. It's eight twenty-five a.m. / It's three forty-five p.m.).

3 Die 24-Stunden-Uhr wird vor allem in Fahrplänen und bei Lautsprecheransagen in Flughäfen und Bahnhöfen angewendet (z. B. The next train for Liverpool will depart at fifteen forty-five). Im Alltag wird sie nicht verwendet, wenn die Tageszeit eindeutig ist. *Five o'clock* heißt meist fünf Uhr nachmittags.

Schreibung und Aussprache

Da sich »Englisch telefonieren leicht gemacht« an den Anfänger mit Vorkenntnissen bzw. den Fortgeschrittenen wendet, soll hier nur kurz auf die wichtigsten Grundregeln zur Aussprache und Schreibung eingegangen werden. Um eine gute und korrekte Aussprache zu erwerben, sollten Sie sich die Texte auf der Begleit-CD möglichst oft anhören. So entwickeln Sie ein Sprachgefühl für die englische Intonation, die im Vergleich zum monotoneren Klang des Deutschen eher einen »Singsang« darstellt.

1 Endet ein Hauptwort auf einen Zischlaut, so wird *-es* angehängt, um die Mehrzahlform zu bilden (z. B. church – churches). Die Endung wird *-iz* gesprochen.
Dieselbe Regel gilt auch für ein Zeitwort, um die 3. Person Einzahl zu bilden (z. B. to wash – he washes).

2 Endet ein Hauptwort auf einen Mitlaut + *-y*, so wird das *-y* zu *-ies*, um die Mehrzahlform zu bilden (z. B. party – parties).
Dieselbe Regel gilt auch für ein Zeitwort, um die 3. Person Einzahl zu bilden (z. B. to marry – he marries).

3 Endet ein Hauptwort auf einen Selbstlaut + *-y*, so bleibt das *-y* in der Mehrzahlform erhalten (z. B. day – days).
Dieselbe Regel gilt auch für ein Zeitwort, um die 3. Person Einzahl zu bilden (z. B. to play – he plays).

4 Endet ein Zeitwort auf *-e*, so entfällt das *-e* in der *-ing*-Form (z. B. to write – writing).

5 Steht in einem Zeitwort ein kurzer, betonter Selbstlaut vor einem Endmitlaut, so wird der Endmitlaut im Partizip verdoppelt (z. B. to sit – sitting; to stop – stopped).

6 Das Alphabet

a = eɪ	j = dʒeɪ	s = es
b = biː	k = keɪ	t = tiː
c = siː	l = el	u = juː
d = diː	m = em	v = viː
e = iː	n = en	w = ˈdʌbljuː
f = ef	o = əʊ	x = eks
g = dʒiː	p = piː	y = waɪ
h = eɪtʃ	q = kjuː	z = zed (US: ziː)
i = aɪ	r = ɑː	

7 Im Englischen wird das *v* wie ein *w* im Deutschen ausgesprochen (z. B. very = "weri"), während das *w* wie *u* und *i* zusammen ausgesprochen wird (z. B. way = "uei").

8 Die Aussprache des *th* sollte am besten vor einem Spiegel geübt werden; es wird mit der Zunge zwischen den Schneidezähnen ausgesprochen: Versuchen Sie, mit der Zunge zwischen den Schneidezähnen »ist« zu sagen. Das klingt wie das so genannte stimmlose *th* in *think* oder *thanks.* Versuchen Sie nun in gleicher Weise »See« zu artikulieren, was dem stimmhaften *th* in *this* und *that* entspricht.

Unit 1: Connecting and Being Connected

Lesen (und hören) Sie den folgenden Dialog:

Switchboard: Good morning, Codex Limited, how can I help you?
Caller: Oh, good morning, David Saunders speaking. Could I speak to John Whiteman, please?
Switchboard: Just one moment, please hold the line.
Caller: Yes, sure.
Switchboard: Mr Saunders, I'm sorry, his line's engaged. Would you like to hold or call back later?
Caller: I'll hold, please.

Some seconds later …

Switchboard: I'm sorry, Mr Saunders, the line's still busy. Do you still want to hold?
Caller: Well, just a little while, then.
Switchboard: Right.

A moment or two later …

Switchboard: The line's free now, Mr Saunders. Shall I put you through?
Caller: Yes, please, thank you.
Switchboard: OK. I'm connecting you now. Goodbye, Mr Saunders.
Caller: Goodbye and thank you.

Wortschatz

Englisch	Deutsch
switchboard	Telefonzentrale
limited ("Ltd")	GmbH
How can I help you?	Wie kann ich Ihnen helfen?
speaking	am Apparat
Could I speak to …?	Könnte ich mit … sprechen?
just one moment	einen Augenblick, bitte
Please hold the line.	Bleiben Sie bitte am Apparat.
His line's engaged.	Seine Leitung ist besetzt.
Would you like to hold?	Möchten Sie warten?
to call back later	später zurückrufen
I'll hold, please.	Ich warte, bitte.

The line's still busy.	Die Leitung ist noch besetzt.
Do you still want to hold?	Wollen Sie noch warten?
just a little while	nur kurz
right	gut; in Ordnung
Shall I put you through?	Soll ich Sie verbinden?
I'm connecting you now.	Ich verbinde Sie jetzt.

A Ergänzen Sie den folgenden Dialog mit den Worten des Anrufers:

Switchboard: Good morning, Codex Limited, how can I help you?

Caller: ....

....

Switchboard: Just one moment, please hold the line.

Caller: ....

Switchboard: Mr Saunders, I'm sorry, his line's engaged. Would you like to hold or call back later?

Caller: ....

Some seconds later …

Switchboard: I'm sorry, Mr Saunders, the line's still busy. Do you still want to hold?

Caller: ....

Switchboard: Right.

A moment or two later …

Switchboard: The line's free now, Mr Saunders. Shall I put you through?

Caller: ....

Switchboard: OK. I'm connecting you now. Goodbye, Mr Saunders.

Caller: ....

Vergleichen Sie Ihre Antworten mit dem Originaltext.

- Hören Sie nun den Übungsdialog Abschnitt für Abschnitt an und sprechen Sie den jeweils gehörten Abschnitt nach.
- Hören Sie nun den Übungsdialog noch einmal (nur Telefonzentrale) und übernehmen Sie die Rolle des Anrufers.

B Setzen Sie die Worte der Telefonzentrale ein, um den folgenden Dialog zu vervollständigen:

Switchboard: ....
Caller: Oh, good morning, David Saunders speaking. Could I speak to John Whiteman, please?

Switchboard: ....
Caller: Yes, sure.

Switchboard: ....
....
Caller: I'll hold, please.
Some seconds later …

Switchboard: ....
....
Caller: Well, just a little while, then.

Switchboard: ....
A moment or two later …

Switchboard: ....
Caller: Yes, please, thank you.

Switchboard: ....
Caller: Goodbye and thank you.

Vergleichen Sie Ihre Antworten mit dem Originaltext.

- Hören Sie den Übungsdialog (nur Anrufer) ein drittes Mal an und übernehmen Sie die Rolle der Telefonzentrale.

Versuchen Sie, den Dialog zu ergänzen, ohne auf den Originaltext zu schauen. Denken Sie daran: Es muss keine genaue Wiedergabe des Originals sein – benutzen Sie Ihr Improvisationstalent!

Dialling Tones

A note on English dialling tones:

- An unbroken, continuous tone means that the line is now free to use.
- Two long tones followed by a pause means that the receiver's phone is ringing.
- Short tones mean that the receiver's line is engaged.
- Fast tones mean that the connection has not been made and should be repeated.

Wortschatz

Englisch	Deutsch
dialling tone	Amtszeichen
continuous	ununterbrochen
tone	Ton
engaged	besetzt; *auch:* verlobt

Übung 1

Ergänzen Sie die folgenden Sätze mit dem passenden **persönlichen Fürwort** oder dem **besitzanzeigenden Fürwort** *(I/me/my/you/your/he/him/his/she/her/it/its/we/us/our/they/them/their)*. Alle Fürwörter können mindestens einmal, einige davon auch mehrmals, gebraucht werden.

1. Switchboard to caller: "Can .... help ...., madam?"
2. Mrs Caxton's busy at present. Would .... like to call .... again later?
3. Shall I give you .... fax number?
4. The partners in London are in a business meeting. Unfortunately, ... cannot be disturbed.
5. I'd like to speak to Gareth Thomson. Is .... line free?
6. Could .... give .... a ring later, please?

7. Deborah Baker has lost .... filofax. Please ask the staff to help .... look for .... It is in .... own case.
8. Give Ronald Walker .... telephone number and ask .... for ....
9. Would .... secretary put .... through to the managing director, please?
10. Sorry, but .... can't make it to the meeting. Please give the members .... apologies.

Siehe Grammatikteil: persönliche Fürwörter und besitzanzeigende Fürwörter, Seite 115. Lösungen zu den Übungen finden Sie ab Seite 122ff.

Wortschatz

Englisch	Deutsch
at present	augenblicklich; zurzeit; im Moment
business meeting	Geschäftssitzung
unfortunately	leider
disturbed	gestört
filofax	eine Art Agendabuch/ Telefonverzeichnis
to look for	suchen
managing director	leitende(r) Direktor(in *f*); Geschäftsführer(in *f*)
to make it	es schaffen; erreichen
member	Mitglied
to give sb. your apologies	sich bei jdm. entschuldigen lassen

The Fax Machine

The modern fax machine has practically replaced the telex machines of the last few decades. The sender can transmit text or pictures to the receiver and has instant confirmation that the documentation has been received. Computers often have a built-in fax modem, whereby the user can send a document that has been generated on-screen straight to the receiver's fax machine.

Englisch	Deutsch
practically	praktisch
to replace	ersetzen
decade	Jahrzehnt
to transmit	senden
receiver	Empfänger(in *f*)
instant	sofortig
confirmation	Bestätigung
to receive	empfangen; erhalten
built-in (or: inbuilt)	eingebaut
whereby	an dem; woran; wonach
user	Benutzer(in *f*)
to generate	erzeugen; entwickeln
straight	direkt; gerade

Fax

The word "fax" is a derivation of the Latin "fac simile", meaning "to make something similar"!

Englisch	Deutsch
derivation	Ableitung
Latin	lateinisch
similar	ähnlich

Übung 2

Ordnen Sie die folgenden Sätze einander zu, die **modale Hilfsverben** *(can/could/may/might/must/need/shall/should/will/would)* enthalten (→ Unit 6).

1. Could I speak to Mrs Wolfe, please?	1	
2. We should hold the meeting in London.	2	
3. The conference might be cancelled.	3	
4. Would you like to hold?	4	
5. You needn't call me back.	5	
6. May I use your telephone?	6	
7. Shall I put you through now?	7	
8. I'll answer the phone!	8	
9. Can I help you, madam?	9	
10. I must be off – thanks for calling.	10	

a. No, I'll call back later.
b. Yes, please.
c. You're welcome. Bye!
d. Of course. Just one moment, please.
e. Certainly. Go ahead.
f. That's a good idea.
g. Oh, that would be a shame.
h. Hurry then!
i. OK, see you at the meeting.
j. Oh, thank you very much.

Siehe Grammatikteil: modale Hilfsverben, Seite 115.
Den Schlüssel zu den Übungen finden Sie ab Seite 122ff.

Wortschatz

Englisch	Deutsch
to hold	veranstalten
to cancel	absagen; fallen lassen
shame	schade
to hurry	sich beeilen
to be off	gehen

Fax Message

You have tried to telephone a business colleague several times this morning, but the line has been engaged. Now you have to leave the office, but you need information on next month's trade exhibition by this evening, so you decide to send a fax, requesting the date and venue of the exhibition.

Complete the following fax message headsheet.

From:

Sender's name: …………… Sender's fax no: ……………

To:

Recipient's name: ………… Recipient's fax no: …………

Date: …………………

Message: ……………………………………………………

……………………………………………………………

……………………………………………………………

……………………………………………………………

……………………………………………………………

……………………………………………………………

……………………………………………………………

Answering the Telephone

When telephoning friends in Great Britain, the first thing that you may hear them say is the telephone number you have just dialled! This is, in fact, quite normal; rather than giving your name, it is common practice to say your own number!

Übung 4

Bilden Sie **Fragen** *(How are you?/Where is he from?/What time do you start work?)* mit den folgenden Wortgruppen (→ Unit 3, 7 und 8).

1. Good morning, Anderton Limited. – How/I/help/you?

   ....?

2. I'm sorry, his line's engaged. – How long/you/want to/wait?

   ....?

3. My fax number is 478 6554. – What/be/yours?

   ....?

4. How much/time/you/need/to write/the report?

   ....?

5. The project meeting is next month. – Where/we/hold/it?

   ....?

Siehe Grammatikteil: Fragen, Seite 115.
Den Schlüssel zu den Übungen finden Sie ab Seite 122ff.

Test

Setzen Sie ein **persönliches**, ein **besitzanzeigendes Fürwort** oder ein **modales Hilfsverb** in die Lücken ein, um den Text zu vervollständigen:

A few weeks ago, I phoned .... colleague, Phil Rogers, who works in York. .... secretary answered and gave .... to understand that Phil was going to get married! She .... not connect me to him at that moment, but .... would ask him to call .... back. Two hours later, Phil phoned; before he .... get a word in edgeways, I cried out "Congratulations! Who's the lucky lady?" There was a stunned silence from Phil's end of the line and an embarrassed one from mine! ".............. secretary told me you were engaged!" I managed to say. Phil has never let .... forget that "engaged" has two meanings and has promised to let me know, ... he ever get "hitched"!

Lösungen zu den Übungen und Tests finden Sie ab Seite 122ff.

Englisch	Deutsch
to get married	heiraten
to get a word in edgeways	überhaupt zu Wort kommen
stunned	sprachlos; fassungslos
embarrassed	verlegen
engaged	verlobt; *auch:* besetzt
to get hitched	heiraten

Unit 2: Leaving and Taking Messages

Lesen (und hören) Sie den folgenden Dialog:

Switchboard: Northcott Hotel, good afternoon. Can I help you?

Nicola Summers: Hello, this is Nicola Summers from Thames Publications. May I speak to the hotel manager, please?

Switchboard: One moment, please, I'll put you through to his personal assistant, Robert Flint.

Nicola Summers: Thank you.

Robert Flint: Hello, Robert Flint speaking.

Nicola Summers: Good afternoon, this is Nicola Summers from Thames Publications. I'd like to speak to the hotel manager, please.

Robert Flint: I'm afraid Mr Chesterton is out all day today. Can I help you at all?

Nicola Summers: Well, could I leave a message for him?

Robert Flint: Yes, of course, please go ahead.

Nicola Summers: We're bringing out a special hotel supplement to accompany our monthly trade journal and would like to feature the Northcott Hotel. If Mr Chesterton is interested, please could he call me back on 0171 875 64 34?

Robert Flint: Right, I've got all that. I'll pass it on to him as soon as he's back.

Nicola Summers: Thank you very much. Goodbye.

Robert Flint: You're welcome. Goodbye Ms Summers.

Wortschatz

Englisch	Deutsch
publication	Publikation; Veröffentlichung
hotel manager	Hotelleiter(in *f*)
personal assistant	Direktionsassistent(in *f*)
I'd like to	ich möchte; ich hätte gern
I'm afraid	es tut mir Leid, aber …; leider
out all day	den ganzen Tag abwesend
at all	irgendwie

Could I leave a message?	Könnte ich eine Nachricht hinterlassen?
Go ahead.	Machen Sie (ruhig) weiter.
to bring out	herausbringen
special	Sonder-
supplement	Beilage
to accompany	begleiten
trade journal	Handelsjournal
to feature	(einen Beitrag) bringen
Could he call me back?	Könnte er mich zurückrufen?
I've got all that.	Das habe ich alles notiert.
I'll pass it on to him.	Ich richte es ihm aus.
as soon as	so bald (wie)
you're welcome	bitte sehr

A Ergänzen Sie den folgenden Dialog mit den Worten von Nicola Summers:

Switchboard: Northcott Hotel, good afternoon. Can I help you?

Nicola Summers: ....

....

Switchboard: One moment, please, I'll put you through to his personal assistant, Robert Flint.

Nicola Summers: ....

Robert Flint: Hello, Robert Flint speaking.

Nicola Summers: ....

....

....

Robert Flint: I'm afraid Mr Chesterton is out all day today. Can I help you at all?

Nicola Summers: ....

Robert Flint: Yes, of course, please go ahead.

Nicola Summers: ....

....

....

....

....

Robert Flint: Right, I've got all that. I'll pass it on to him as soon as he's back.

Nicola Summers: ....

Robert Flint: You're welcome. Goodbye Ms Summers.

Vergleichen Sie Ihre Antworten mit dem Originaltext.

- Hören Sie nun den Übungsdialog Abschnitt für Abschnitt an und sprechen Sie den jeweils gehörten Abschnitt nach.
- Hören Sie den Übungsdialog noch einmal an (nur Telefonzentrale und Robert Flint) und übernehmen Sie die Rolle von Nicola Summers.

B Ergänzen Sie den folgenden Dialog mit den Worten der Telefonzentrale und von Robert Flint:

Switchboard: ....

Nicola Summers: Hello, this is Nicola Summers from Thames Publications. May I speak to the hotel manager, please?

Switchboard: ....

....

Nicola Summers: Thank you.

Robert Flint: ....

Nicola Summers: Good afternoon, this is Nicola Summers from Thames Publications. I'd like to speak to the hotel manager, please.

Robert Flint: ....

....

Nicola Summers: Well, could I leave a message for him?

Robert Flint: ....

Nicola Summers: We're bringing out a special hotel supplement to accompany our monthly trade journal and would like to feature the Northcott Hotel. If Mr Chesterton is interested, please could he call me back on 0171 875 64 34?

Robert Flint: ....

....

Nicola Summers: Thank you very much. Goodbye.

Robert Flint: You're welcome. Goodbye Ms Summers.

Vergleichen Sie Ihre Antworten mit dem Originaltext.

- Hören Sie den Übungsdialog ein drittes Mal an (nur Nicola Summers) und übernehmen Sie die Rolle der Telefonzentrale und die von Robert Flint.

Versuchen Sie, den Dialog zu ergänzen, ohne auf die Originaltexte zu schauen. Denken Sie daran: Es muss keine genaue Wiedergabe des Originals sein – benutzen Sie Ihr Improvisationstalent!

Telephone Alphabet

A	Alfred (or Andrew)	N	Nellie
B	Benjamin	O	Oliver
C	Charles (or Charlie)	P	Peter
D	David	Q	Queen (or Queenie)
E	Edward	R	Robert
F	Frederick	S	Samuel (or Sugar)
G	George	T	Tommy
H	Harry	U	Uncle
I	Isaac	V	Victor
J	Jack	W	William
K	King	X	X-ray
L	London (or Lussy)	Y	Yellow
M	Mary	Z	Zebra

Übung 1

Wählen Sie das richtige **Verhältniswort** *(at/by/for/from/in/of/on/through/to/until)* für die folgenden Sätze (→ Unit 5).

1. Can I speak .... Mr Browning?
2. Please call me .... 0181 578 93 72.
3. Would you like a list .... phone numbers?
4. Ms Reed is .... a conference.
5. Are you interested .... joining us?
6. Could you arrange an appointment .... me?
7. We must decide .... Friday!
8. There's a message .... Derek.
9. Put me .... to the personnel department.
10. I'm working .... six today.

▶ Siehe Grammatikteil: Verhältniswörter, Seite 116.

Wortschatz

Englisch	Deutsch
conference	Konferenz
to join	sich anschließen; beitreten
appointment	Termin; Verabredung
to decide	sich entscheiden
personnel department	Personalabteilung

Telephone Etiquette

Telephone manners – a very important part of telephoning today. Be polite, speak clearly and identify yourself immediately. Know what you are going to say before you even dial the other person's number and keep it in mind whether you are making a social or a business call. Never assume you know who is going to answer the phone – you may be in for an unexpected surprise!

Englisch	Deutsch
manners	Sitten (und Gebräuche)
polite	höflich
clearly	klar; deutlich
to identify yourself	sich ausweisen; sich identifizieren
immediately	sofort
even	sogar; selbst
to dial	(eine Nummer) wählen
to keep sth. in mind	etwas im Auge behalten
whether … or	ob … oder
to assume	annehmen
you may be in for sth.	du kannst dich auf etwas gefasst machen
unexpected	unerwartet
surprise	Überraschung

Local Calls in the USA

Local calls are free of charge in many parts of the USA, so be sure to enquire at the relevant tourist office!

Englisch	Deutsch
local	lokal; Orts-
free of charge	kostenlos; gratis
to enquire/inquire about sth.	sich nach etwas erkundigen
relevant	zuständig

Übung 2

Wählen Sie die richtige **Gegenwartsform** *(I write/I am writing)* (→ Unit 10).

1. Ms White (**is talking/talks**) on the phone right now.
2. Mark Andrews (**dictates/is dictating**) letters to his secretary every Monday morning.
3. I (**connect/am connecting**) you now, Mr Saunders.
4. Debbie (**doesn't come in/isn't coming in**) on Fridays, I'm afraid.
5. We (**aren't bringing/don't bring**) out a special supplement for Christmas this year.
6. You (**never speak/are never speaking**) clearly enough on the telephone, Andy.
7. Where (**are you holding/do you hold**) the meeting this year?
8. When (**does Annie start/is Annie starting**) work in the mornings?
9. (**Are you sending/Do you send**) that e-mail to Winterson Ltd, Susan?
10. (**Do they ever answer/Are they ever answering**) our faxes?

Siehe Grammatikteil: Gegenwartsformen, Seite 116.

Wortschatz

Englisch	Deutsch
to dictate	diktieren
Christmas	Weihnachten
enough	genug; genügend

Übung 3

Telephone Message

There is a phone call for a colleague who is not in the office today. The caller would like to discuss proposals for a new project and asks for your colleague to call her back as soon as possible. Take the imaginary message.

Date: .... Time: ....

Caller's name: ....

Caller's number: ....

Message: ....

....

....

....

....

....

Social Calling Hours

These vary, depending on how well you know the person you are calling! Generally, telephoning between 9 a.m. and 9 p.m. is acceptable, though it's probably prudent to call a little later in the morning at weekends!

Wortschatz

Englisch	Deutsch
social calling hours	Anrufzeiten
to vary	sich unterscheiden; abweichen
to depend on sth.	abhängen von etwas
prudent	wohl überlegt

Übung 4

Setzen Sie ein passendes **Bestimmungswort** *(the/a(n)/this/that/these/those)* in die Lücken ein:

1. Could I make .... quick phone call, please?
2. .... phones over there are all in use at present.
3. .... line here is free now. Shall I put you through?
4. The partners are over in London at .... meeting about .... new project.
5. Angela, would you send .... memo to Mr Greenaway, please?
6. I've just received .... graphics here. What do you think of them, Andrew?
7. .... is a very nice surprise! Thank you for .... present, Eleanor!
8. Good morning, ... is Carolyn Little from Caxford Holdings.
9. Shall I send you .... e-mail?
10. .... are the telephone numbers you wanted, Mrs Fox.

▶ Siehe Grammatikteil: Bestimmungswörter, Seite 116.

Wortschatz

Englisch	**Deutsch**
memo (= memorandum)	Mitteilung; Notiz
graphics	Zeichnungen
present	Geschenk
holdings	Gutsbesitz

Verneinen Sie die unterstrichenen Satzteile:

It was (..............) a normal Monday morning. Terry, my new secretary, was (..............) at his desk as usual. I sat (..............) down and answered (..............) my messages. Some were (..............) very interesting, for example, "Congratulations – good secretary!" and "Great little assistant!" But the one from David Bankes, over at Purchasing, really was (..............) very amusing: "Sarah, could (..............) I borrow your secretary – I might (..............) let you have her back, though, after a lunchtime drink!" Terry laughed (..............), but said (..............) he would (..............) go!

Englisch	Deutsch
as usual	wie üblich; wie gewöhnlich
Purchasing	Einkauf(sabteilung)
amusing	lustig
to borrow	borgen; ausleihen
though	jedoch; obwohl
to laugh	lachen

Siehe Grammatikteil: Negation, Seite 117.

Unit 3: Requesting Information

Lesen (und hören) Sie den folgenden Dialog:

Personal Assistant: Ken Jackson's personal assistant speaking. How can I help you?
Amanda Gray: Yes, it's Amanda Gray. Could I speak to Ken, please?
Personal Assistant: Just one moment, I'll see if he's available.
A few moments later …
Personal Assistant: OK, I'm putting you through now.
Amanda Gray: Thank you.
Ken Jackson: Hello, Amanda. How are you?
Amanda Gray: Fine, and yourself?
Ken Jackson: Fine – busy as usual! Now, what can I do for you?
Amanda Gray: Well, I was wondering if you could let me have some information about the new marketing proposals.
Ken Jackson: We're not quite that far ahead yet; at present we've only outlined a few ideas and discussed one or two suggestions. It's also still quite confidential, but as soon as we have anything concrete, I'll let you know.
Amanda Gray: That would be super. Thanks a lot.
Ken Jackson: It's a pleasure. How's the family, by the way?
Amanda Gray: They're all fine, thank you. And yours?
Ken Jackson: Likewise. We must meet up for a drink sometime.
Amanda Gray: Yes, let's. Well, bye for now, Ken.
Ken Jackson: Bye. Thanks for calling.

Wortschatz

Englisch	**Deutsch**
personal assistant	Direktionsassistent(in *f*)
available	frei; verfügbar; *auch:* erhältlich
busy	beschäftigt
as usual	wie üblich; wie gewöhnlich
to wonder	sich fragen

proposal	Vorschlag
quite	ganz; *auch:* ziemlich
far ahead	(weit) voraus
at present	augenblicklich; zurzeit; im Moment; im Augenblick
to outline	umreißen; skizzieren
to discuss	besprechen
suggestion	Vorschlag
confidential	vertraulich
concrete	konkret
pleasure	Vergnügen
by the way	übrigens
likewise	ebenso; gleichermaßen
to meet up	sich treffen
sometime	irgendwann
let's (= let us do that)	oh ja; gern
bye for now	bis bald

A Setzen Sie in den folgenden Dialog die Worte von Amanda Gray ein:

Personal Assistant: Ken Jackson's personal assistant speaking. How can I help you?

Amanda Gray: ....

Personal Assistant: Just one moment, I'll see if he's available.

A few moments later …

Personal Assistant: OK, I'm putting you through now.

Amanda Gray: ....

Ken Jackson: Hello, Amanda. How are you?

Amanda Gray: ....

Ken Jackson: Fine – busy as usual! Now, what can I do for you?

Amanda Gray: ....

....

....

Ken Jackson: We're not quite that far ahead; at present we've only outlined a few ideas and discussed one or two suggestions. It's also still quite confidential, but as soon as we have anything concrete, I'll let you know.

Amanda Gray: ....

Ken Jackson: It's a pleasure. How's the family, by the way?

Amanda Gray: ....

Ken Jackson: Likewise. We must meet up for a drink sometime.

Amanda Gray: ....

Ken Jackson: Bye. Thanks for calling.

Vergleichen Sie Ihre Antworten mit dem Originaltext.

- Hören Sie nun den Übungsdialog Abschnitt für Abschnitt an und sprechen Sie den jeweils gehörten Abschnitt nach.
- Hören Sie den Übungsdialog noch einmal an (nur Direktionsassistent und Ken Jackson) und übernehmen Sie die Rolle von Amanda Gray.

B Ergänzen Sie den folgenden Dialog mit den Worten des Direktionsassistenten und denen von Ken Jackson:

Personal Assistant: ....

....

Amanda Gray: Yes, it's Amanda Gray. Could I speak to Ken, please?

Personal Assistant: ....

A few moments later …

Personal Assistant: ....

Amanda Gray: Thank you.

Ken Jackson: ....

Amanda Gray: Fine, and yourself?

Ken Jackson: ....

Amanda Gray: Well, I was wondering if you could let me have some information about the new marketing proposals.

Ken Jackson: ....

....

....

....

....

Amanda Gray: That would be super. Thanks a lot.

Ken Jackson: ....

Amanda Gray: They're all fine, thank you. And yours?

Ken Jackson: ....

Amanda Gray: Yes, let's. Well, bye for now, Ken.

Ken Jackson: ....

Vergleichen Sie Ihre Antworten mit dem Originaltext.

- Hören Sie den Übungsdialog ein drittes Mal an (nur Amanda Gray) und übernehmen Sie die Rolle des Direktionsassistenten und die von Ken Jackson.

Versuchen Sie, den Dialog zu ergänzen, ohne auf die Originaltexte zu schauen. Benutzen Sie Ihr Improvisationstalent!

Muzak "Muzak" is the trademark name given to the recorded playing of light music in shops and, more recently, on telephones, while you are waiting to be connected.

Englisch	Deutsch
Muzak	Berieselungsmusik
trademark	Warenzeichen
recorded	aufgezeichnet
recently	kürzlich; vor kurzem

Übung 1

Wählen Sie das richtige Zeitwort in der **Befehlsform** *(answer/call/go/hold/put/ring/send/shout/use/worry)* und setzen Sie es in die Lücken (→ Unit 9) ein.

1. .... the other phone, would you?
2. .... me through to accounts, please.
3. Please .... ahead.
4. .... that fax to personnel, please, Ms Williams.
5. .... the line, please.
6. Don't .... about finishing the report today, Peter.
7. Please don't .... my telephone for private calls.
8. Don't .... her on her direct line, please.
9. Please don't .... – I can hear you perfectly well.
10. Don't .... us; we'll call you!

Siehe Grammatikteil: Befehlsform, Seite 117.

Wortschatz

Englisch	Deutsch
accounts	Buchhaltung
personnel	Personal(abteilung)
to worry	sich sorgen; sich Gedanken machen
direct line	Durchwahlnummer
to shout	rufen; schreien; brüllen

The Telephone Answering Machine

Answering machines come in many forms today; there are personal answering machines, answering services and fax link-ups. You may record your own personal message or use a system greeting. Most users are now reconciled to leaving messages, though there are still a few die-hards who resist speaking into what seems to be thin air!

Englisch	Deutsch
service	Dienst; Dienstleistung
link-up	Verbindung
to record	(Tonband-)Aufnahmen machen
message	Nachricht
greeting	Begrüßung
to be reconciled to sth.	sich mit etwas versöhnen
though	jedoch; obwohl
die-hard	Ewiggestrige(r)
to resist	sich widersetzen
thin air	nichts

Abbreviations

asap	as soon as possible
BT	British Telecom
swbd	switchboard
STD	subscriber trunk dialling
T	telephone (found on maps)
tel	telephone
tel no	telephone number

Englisch	Deutsch
abbreviation	Abkürzung
as soon as possible	so bald wie möglich
subscriber trunk dialling	Selbstwählferndienst
map	(Land-)Karte; Stadtplan

Übung 2

Setzen Sie die richtige **Zukunftsform** *(I will write/I am going to write)* in die Lücken ein (→ Unit 10).

1. Please answer the other phone – it .... be Tanson Holdings!
2. Look out! You .... drop that file!
3. You've typed the wrong letter, Mr Marshall. – I'm so sorry; I .... do it again immediately, Mrs Soames.
4. Would you like to hold or call back later? – I .... hold, please.
5. Rosemary told me you're taking a computer course. – That's right. I .... start tonight, actually.
6. Oh, no! Look at the fax machine! It .... run out of paper!
7. Would you like to practise sending an e-mail, Miss Simpson? – Yes, all right. I .... try!
8. I don't think the computer is working properly. I've a feeling it .... crash at any moment.
9. The phone's ringing, Diane. – OK, I .... answer it.
10. I hear you're leaving us, Rebecca. – Yes, I .... take a year off and travel around the world.

▶ Siehe Grammatikteil: Zukunftsformen, Seite 119f.

Englisch	Deutsch
to drop	fallen lassen
file	Ordner
immediately	sofort
actually	eigentlich
to run out	ablaufen; ausgehen; zu Ende gehen
to practise	üben
to crash	abstürzen

Answering Machine Message

You phone a business contact in another firm to arrange a meeting over lunch next week. He does not answer, so you leave a message on his answering machine, suggesting a date and a place and asking him to call you back. Write what you would say.

Useful Telephone Numbers

- Emergencies: (Fire, Police, Ambulance, Coast Guard, Mountain Rescue, Cave Rescue) — 999 (or 112)
- Operator Services — 100
- Directory Enquiries — 192
- International Numbers — 153
- Fault Reporting — 151

Wortschatz

Englisch	Deutsch
emergency	Notfall
ambulance	Krankenwagen
coast guard	Küstenwache
mountain, cave rescue	Berg-, Höhlenrettungsdienst
directory enquiries	Auskunft
fault reporting	Störungsdienst

Übung 4

Setzen Sie ein **Fragewort** *(who/where/why/how long/how much/how many/when/what/which)* ein, um die folgenden Fragen zu vervollständigen (→ Unit 1, 7 und 8).

1. Good morning. .... can I help you?
2. .... is the meeting going to take place? – Next month, I think.
3. .... are you phoning from, Simon? – From a call box at Piccadilly Circus!
4. .... do you prefer – fax or e-mail? I don't know, really – they both have advantages and disadvantages.
5. .... will it take you to type the letter, Phil? – I need about an hour.
6. .... can I do for you, Mr Bridges?
7. .... phone lines do you have? – Five business, and one private.
8. .... are you restructuring? – Because the business is expanding and we would like to create more job opportunities.
9. .... is in charge today? – The deputy manager.
10. .... can you afford to spend on project planning?

▶ Siehe Grammatikteil: Fragen, Seite 115.

Englisch	Deutsch
call box	Telefonzelle
to prefer	vorziehen; bevorzugen
advantage	Vorteil
disadvantage	Nachteil
to expand	erweitern; expandieren
to create	(er)schaffen
opportunity	Gelegenheit; Möglichkeit
to be in charge	verantwortlich sein
deputy manager	stellvertretende(r) Betriebsleiter(in *f*)
to afford	sich leisten
to spend	(Geld) ausgeben

Wählen Sie die richtige Antwort, um die Sätze zu vervollständigen:

1. Could you let me have some .... about the new proposals?

   a) presents b) accounts c) information

2. I'm sorry, it's still rather .... at present.

   a) interested b) confidential c) available

3. The supplement will .... the trade journal.

   a) accompany b) decide c) engage

4. Would you connect me, now? .... Mr Mitchell.

   a) Unfortunately, b) Certainly, c) Clearly,

5. What are your plans? Please .... them.

   a) wonder b) hold c) outline

Unit 4: Project Planning

Lesen (und hören) Sie den folgenden Dialog:

Alex Bell: So, Angie, how's it going?

Angie Clarke: Rushed off our feet – as always!

Alex Bell: Have you had a chance to think about Project One?

Angie Clarke: Yes. In fact, I've drawn up a list of strategies, which we can discuss at length at the next meeting.

Alex Bell: Great. What have you based the strategies on?

Angie Clarke: On the ideas we talked about last time and on the basic concepts your firm outlined to us.

Alex Bell: Sounds good, Angie. Could you tell me briefly what sort of strategies you think would be worthwhile?

Angie Clarke: Sure. Well, I've put them under general headings, as follows: Financing; Recruitment; Briefing; Implementation; Outcome.

Alex Bell: OK. Financing and Recruitment will be handled by Accounts and Personnel, so I'll arrange a meeting with the respective heads of department. Briefing and Implementation will be carried out by my department …

Angie Clarke: … and let's hope for a successful outcome!

Alex Bell: I'm sure it will be.

Angie Clarke: Alex, I'm really sorry, but I have to be off. Can we discuss this further tomorrow?

Alex Bell: Yes, sure. Goodbye Angie.

Angie Clarke: Bye!

Wortschatz

Englisch	Deutsch
to be rushed off one's feet	dauernd auf Trab sein
as always	wie immer
to draw up	aufsetzen; aufstellen
strategy	Strategie
at length	lange; ausführlich
to base on sth.	basieren auf etwas

concept	Idee; Konzept
firm	Firma
to sound	klingen; tönen
briefly	kurz
worthwhile	lohnend
heading	Stichwort; Rubrik
as follows	wie folgt
recruitment	Einstellung
briefing	Instruktionen; Anweisungen
implementation	Ausführung
outcome	Ergebnis
to handle	erledigen; bearbeiten
respective	jeweilig
successful	erfolgreich
to be off	gehen
further	weiter

A Ergänzen Sie die Worte von Angie Clarke im folgenden Dialog:

Alex Bell: So, Angie, how's it going?

Angie Clarke: ....

Alex Bell: Have you had a chance to think about Project One?

Angie Clarke: ....

....

Alex Bell: Great. What have you based the strategies on?

Angie Clarke: ....

....

Alex Bell: Sounds good, Angie. Could you tell me briefly what sort of strategies you think would be worthwhile?

Angie Clarke: ....

....

....

Alex Bell: OK. Financing and Recruitment will be handled by Accounts and Personnel, so I'll arrange a meeting with the respective heads of department. Briefing and Implementation will be carried out by my department ...

Angie Clarke: ....

Alex Bell: I'm sure it will be.

Angie Clarke: ....

....

Alex Bell: Yes, sure. Goodbye Angie.

Angie Clarke: ....

Vergleichen Sie Ihre Antworten mit dem Originaltext.

- Hören Sie nun den Übungsdialog Abschnitt für Abschnitt an und sprechen Sie den jeweils gehörten Abschnitt nach.
- Hören Sie den Übungsdialog noch einmal an (nur Alex Bell) und übernehmen Sie die Rolle von Angie Clarke.

B Ergänzen Sie in folgendem Dialog die Worte von Alex Bell:

Alex Bell: ....

Angie Clarke: Rushed off our feet – as always!

Alex Bell: ....

Angie Clarke: Yes. In fact, I've drawn up a list of strategies, which we can discuss at length at the next meeting.

Alex Bell: ....

Angie Clarke: On the ideas we talked about last time and on the basic concepts your firm outlined to us.

Alex Bell: ....

....

....

Angie Clarke: Sure. Well, I've put them under general headings, as follows: Financing; Recruitment; Briefing; Implementation; Outcome.

Alex Bell: ....

....

....

....

....

Angie Clarke: … and let's hope for a successful outcome!

Alex Bell: ....

Angie Clarke: Alex, I'm really sorry, but I have to be off. Can we discuss this further tomorrow?

Alex Bell: ....

Angie Clarke: Bye!

Vergleichen Sie Ihre Antworten mit dem Originaltext.

- Hören Sie den Übungsdialog ein drittes Mal an (nur Angie Clarke) und übernehmen Sie die Rolle von Alex Bell.

Versuchen Sie, den Dialog zu ergänzen, ohne auf die Originaltexte zu schauen. Denken Sie daran: Es muss keine genaue Wiedergabe des Originals sein – benutzen Sie Ihr Improvisationstalent!

Titles

Mr = (pronounced "mister") Used before the name of a married or unmarried man.

Mrs = (pronounced "missiz") Used before the name of a married woman.

Miss = used before the name of an unmarried woman.

Ms = (pronounced variously as "miz" or "muz") Used before the name of a married or unmarried woman.

Messrs = (pronounced "messers") Used before the names of two or more partners in the title of a firm or company.

Wortschatz

Englisch	Deutsch
title	Anrede
pronounced	ausgesprochen
used	gebraucht; angewendet
(un)married	(un)verheiratet
variously	verschiedentlich

Übung 1

Setzen Sie die richtige Form des **einfachen Imperfekts** *(I wrote/ she looked)* ein (→ Unit 10).

1. Mrs Anderson (be) .... at a conference last week.
2. Joe (phone) .... a colleague to find out what the company's strategies (be) ....
3. Messrs Charlton (handle) .... the publicity pertaining to the new project.
4. Mr Beck's personal assistant (write) .... down the details of the initial project planning.
5. We (run) .... out of fax paper this morning.
6. When .... you (send) .... that e-mail, Kathy?
7. .... you (speak) .... to Nicholas Campbell about the meeting?
8. I .... n't (answer) .... any of the messages yesterday morning.
9. Jeremy .... n't (see) .... the concept outlines, did he?
10. They (be) .... not very far ahead with the planning.

Siehe Grammatikteil: einfaches Imperfekt, Seite 118.

Englisch	Deutsch
colleague	Arbeitskollege(in *f*)
pertaining to	betreffend
initial	anfänglich
outline	Umriss

To Telephone or Not to Telephone?

The days of just popping round to a friend's house are over. The pace of life is such that like appointments, casual visits must also generally be booked in advance – and confirmed – by phone! Almost everyone has a telephone these days, and the increase in mobile phones makes it easier than ever to catch another person and conduct all social arrangements over the air.

Englisch	Deutsch
to pop round	kurz vorbeikommen; vorbeischauen
over	vorbei; zu Ende
pace	Tempo
nearly; almost	fast; beinahe
appointment	Termin; Verabredung
casual	informell
in advance	im Voraus
increase	Zunahme; Steigerung
mobile phone	Handy; Mobiltelefon
to catch	erwischen
to conduct	führen
arrangement	Abmachung; Verabredung

OFTEL After British Telecom, or “BT”, was privatised, the Government set up an independent body, the Office of Telecommunications, or “OFTEL”, to act as a watchdog organisation and oversee the telephone service. Subscribers can refer a complaint to OFTEL if they are unhappy with the way the telephone service has handled their case.

Wortschatz

Englisch	Deutsch
to privatise	privatisieren
government	Regierung
independent	unabhängig, selbstständig
body	Organ
to act	handeln; unternehmen
watchdog	Wachhund; Wächter; Überwachungsbeauftragte(r)
oversee	beaufsichtigen; überwachen
subscriber	Teilnehmer(in *f*); Abonnent(in *f*)
to refer	weiterleiten
complaint	Beschwerde; Klage
case	Fall

Übung 2

Setzen Sie die richtige Form von *there is/there are* ein, um die folgenden Sätze zu vervollständigen. Sie können auch die Vergangenheitsform benutzen.

1. There .... a call for you, Mrs Charlton. – OK, I’ll take it now.
2. When’s the next meeting? There .... a few points pertaining to the new project which we still have to discuss.
3. There .... some messages on your answering machine this morning, but nothing very important.
4. Sally, there .... a call from Martin Beadle a few minutes ago.

5. Unfortunately, there ....n't a direct line to the Chairman at present.
6. The meeting was a total failure, Jim! There ....n't any worthwhile suggestions at all.
7. .... there any chance of some information about your company's latest plans for restructuring?
8. .... there enough coffee for all the conference delegates yesterday?

Siehe Grammatikteil: *there is/there are,* Seite 118f.

Wortschatz

Englisch	**Deutsch**
a few minutes ago	vor ein paar Minuten
failure	Misserfolg
worthwile	lohnend; der Mühe wert
latest	neueste(r)

Übung 3

Telephone Message

Hören Sie die telefonische Nachricht an und füllen Sie die Lücken im unten stehenden Text.

"Tim – just a quick call – we're .... the first meeting next week to .... the new project – we need all the heads of .... to be present. Could you send out a .... asking them to get a few ideas down on paper: .... will be in charge of new .... and ...., Finance will look after ...., Purchasing will be .... for buying new stock and .... will handle publicity. Have you got all that? Great! Thanks and speak to you soon. Bye!"

The Yellow Pages

The "Yellow Pages" is a well-known guide to local businesses, trade associations and professional bodies. It also contains information about council departments and general facilities in the region.

Wortschatz

Englisch	**Deutsch**
The Yellow Pages	Die Gelben Seiten
well-known	bekannt
guide	Führer
trade association	Handelsverband
professional body	Körperschaft
council	Gemeinde
facility	Einrichtung

Übung 4

Benutzen Sie das **einfache Perfekt** *(I have written/he has looked)*, um die Sätze zu vervollständigen (→ Unit 10).

1. Linda (book) .... your hotel room for you already.
2. We (receive) .... just .... the new proposals.
3. Mike Edwards (forget) .... about the staff meeting!
4. I (lose) .... Ben Challen's new phone number.
5. Chris and I (outline) .... not .... any plans yet.
6. The boss (give) .... not .... us any information about the Anglo Project!
7. .... you (return) .... John's call?
8. .... she (tell) .... her colleagues about the phone call?

9. Where .... you (be) .... ? There's a lot of work waiting for you!

10. What .... Oliver Richards (do) .... about that e-mail?

Siehe Grammatikteil: einfaches Perfekt, Seite 118.

Wortschatz

Englisch	Deutsch
to book	buchen; reservieren
to receive	empfangen; erhalten
staff meeting	Personalsitzung
to return a call	zurückrufen

Test

Ergänzen Sie den folgenden Text mit dem passenden Wort. Die drei Anfangsbuchstaben sind jeweils vorgegeben:

“Hello, Liz, how are you? Fine? Good! I haven't got much time, so I just want to bri................. give you a few details per................. to our new str................., as fol..............: I'm dea.............. with the imp.............. of the con................. plan, the Finance Dep................. will han.............. budgeting, Personnel is in cha.............. of the rec................. of new staff, and I'd like you to make arr................. for a staff mee................. . OK? Let's hope the out................. will be a suc................. one! Thanks a lot, bye for now.”

Wortschatz

Englisch	Deutsch
detail	Einzelheit; Detail
budgeting	Budget
Personnel	Personal(abteilung)
staff	Personal

Unit 5: Organizing

Lesen (und hören) Sie den folgenden Dialog:

Carol Hopkins: Hello, Paul. Glad I caught you!
Paul Norman: Hi, Carol. Yes, you're lucky – I was just on my way out!
Carol Hopkins: Well, I won't keep you long. I just wanted to fix a date for the first meeting. We've briefed our departments and expect some feedback pretty soon.
Paul Norman: OK. The deadline is February next year, isn't it?
Carol Hopkins: Yes, that's right. The trade fair is at the beginning of March and we must be ready by then.
Paul Norman: I think the best thing would be to have the first meeting, which will be rather general, two weeks today at ten o'clock.
Carol Hopkins: What about further meetings after that?
Paul Norman: I would say every month, so that we can implement the four phases of the project consecutively.
Carol Hopkins: I'm not sure if that's very realistic. A lot of the staff are on holiday during the summer. What about having the meetings every two months?
Paul Norman: Well … let's compromise and say every six weeks.
Carol Hopkins: Done! I'll inform my team accordingly.
Paul Norman: Me too. Right, I look forward to seeing you in two weeks. Thanks for ringing.
Carol Hopkins: My pleasure. Have a good weekend.

Englisch	Deutsch
glad	froh
to catch	erwischen
to be lucky	Glück haben
to fix a date	einen Termin festlegen
feedback	Feedback; Reaktion
pretty	ziemlich
deadline	(letzter) Termin
trade fair	Handelsmesse
ready	fertig; bereit
two weeks today	heute in zwei Wochen
to implement	durchführen; ausführen
consecutively	nacheinander; hintereinander
realistic	realistisch
to compromise	einen Kompromiss schließen
Done!	Abgemacht!
accordingly	(dem)entsprechend
to look forward to doing sth.	sich darauf freuen, etwas zu tun

A Setzen Sie in den folgenden Dialog die Worte des Anrufers ein:

Carol Hopkins: Hello, Paul. Glad I caught you!

Paul Norman: ....

....

Carol Hopkins: Well, I won't keep you long. I just wanted to fix a date for the first meeting. We've briefed our departments and expect some feedback pretty soon.

Paul Norman: ....

Carol Hopkins: Yes, that's right. The trade fair is at the beginning of March and we must be ready by then.

Paul Norman: ....

....

....

Carol Hopkins: What about further meetings after that?

Paul Norman: ……………………………………………

……………………………………………

Carol Hopkins: I'm not sure if that's very realistic. A lot of the staff are on holiday during the summer. What about having the meetings every two months?

Paul Norman: ……………………………………………

Carol Hopkins: Done! I'll inform my team accordingly.

Paul Norman: ……………………………………………

……………………………………………

Carol Hopkins: My pleasure. Have a good weekend.

Vergleichen Sie Ihre Antworten mit dem Originaltext.

- Hören Sie nun den Übungsdialog Abschnitt für Abschnitt an und sprechen Sie den jeweils gehörten Abschnitt nach.
- Hören Sie den Übungsdialog noch einmal an (nur Carol Hopkins) und übernehmen Sie die Rolle von Paul Norman.

B Ergänzen Sie die Worte von Carol Hopkins im folgenden Dialog:

Carol Hopkins: ……………………………………………

Paul Norman: Hi, Carol. Yes, you're lucky – I was just on my way out!

Carol Hopkins: ……………………………………………

……………………………………………

……………………………………………

……………………………………………

Paul Norman: OK. The deadline is February next year, isn't it?

Carol Hopkins: ……………………………………………

……………………………………………

Paul Norman: I think the best thing would be to have the first meeting, which will be rather general, two weeks today at ten o'clock.

Carol Hopkins: ……………………………………………
Paul Norman: I would say every month, so that we can implement the four phases of the project consecutively.

Carol Hopkins: ……………………………………………

……………………………………………

……………………………………………

Paul Norman: Well … let's compromise and say every six weeks.

Carol Hopkins: ……………………………………………
Paul Norman: Me too. Right, I look forward to seeing you in two weeks. Thanks for ringing.

Carol Hopkins: ……………………………………………

Vergleichen Sie Ihre Antworten mit dem Originaltext.

- Hören Sie den Übungsdialog ein drittes Mal an (nur Paul Norman) und übernehmen Sie die Rolle von Carol Hopkins.

Versuchen Sie, den Dialog zu ergänzen, ohne auf die Originaltexte zu schauen. Übrigens: Es muss keine genaue Wiedergabe des Originals sein, benutzen Sie Ihr Improvisationstalent!

Greetings and Goodbyes

Greetings	Goodbyes		
Hi!	Cheers! Cheerio!	=	Informal, usually between people who know each other well.
Hello!	Bye!	=	Both formal and informal.
Good morning/ afternoon!	Goodbye!	=	Formal.

Übung 1

Vervollständigen Sie die folgenden Sätze mit **some** oder **any**.

1. Here's .... information regarding the trade fair, Teresa.
2. We haven't had .... feedback yet.
3. Are there .... messages for me? – No, not today, I'm afraid.
4. Is there .... more news about the takeover?
5. I'd like .... positive comments from the staff.
6. They don't have .... free telephone lines at the moment.
7. When can you do .... typing for me, Gary?
8. Why can't we find .... temporary secretaries?

▶ Siehe Grammatikteil: *some* und *any*, Seite 119.

Wortschatz

Englisch	Deutsch
regarding	betreffend; über
takeover	Übernahme
comment	Bemerkung
temporary	vorübergehend; Aushilfs-

Formal versus Informal

Private telephone calls tend to be a lot more casual than business calls, a fact reflected in the language used. People say "Hi!" rather than "Good morning!" and "Cheers!" instead of "Goodbye!". Nevertheless, the same rules of etiquette apply, whether you are enquiring about a post you have seen advertised, or phoning your best friend for a chat. Common courtesy is the order of the day.

Englisch	Deutsch
versus	gegen
to tend	neigen; tendieren
casual	zwanglos; ungezwungen
rather than	eher als
instead of	statt; anstelle von
nevertheless	trotzdem
to apply	gelten
to enquire/inquire about sth.	sich nach etwas erkundigen
advertised	ausgeschrieben
chat	Plauderei; Schwatz
courtesy	Höflichkeit
to be the order of the day	auf der Tagesordnung stehen

Helplines

There are now more national telephone "helplines" than ever before, ranging from animal welfare, through gambling, to smoking. All offer confidential advice or counselling, and many are free of charge.

Englisch	Deutsch
helpline	telefonische Hilfen
to range from … to …	von … bis … reichen
welfare	Fürsorge
gambling	Spielen; Wetten
advice	Rat(schlag)
counselling	Beratung
free of charge	kostenlos; gratis

Übung 2

Setzen Sie die alternative Form der **Uhrzeit** *(e.g. 7.40 p.m. = twenty to eight in the evening)* ein, um die Sätze zu vervollständigen (→ Unit 8).

1. It's 2.15 p.m. That means it's:

   ....

2. It's 7.30 a.m. That means it's:

   ....

3. It's 11 p.m. That means it's:

   ....

4. It's 9.45 a.m. That means it's:

   ....

5. It's 6 p.m. That means it's:

   ....

6. It's 12.10 p.m. That means it's:

   ....

7. It's 6.25 a.m. That means it's:

   ....

8. It's 3.35 p.m. That means it's:

   ....

9. It's 10.50 a.m. That means it's:

   ....

10. It's 11.59 p.m. That means it's:

    ....

▶ Siehe wichtige Grundbegriffe: Uhrzeit, Seite 9.

Imaginary Letter

You wish to meet your business partner in London to discuss the deadlines for a new project. Write an imaginary letter to her, suggesting a place, date and time for a meeting, and outlining the main points to be discussed.

....

....

....

....

....

Abbreviations

GMT	Greenwich Mean (or: Meridian Time)
ETA	estimated time of arrival
OFTEL	Office of Telecommunications
ODETTE	Organization for Data Exchange through Tele-Transmission in Europe
Plc	public limited company
UK	United Kingdom
USA	United States of America

Englisch	Deutsch
estimated time of arrival	geschätzte Ankunft
telecommunications	Fernmeldewesen
through	durch
public limited company	Aktiengesellschaft

Übung 4

Setzen Sie das richtige **Verhältniswort** in folgende Sätze ein (→ Unit 2).

1. Could you give me some information .... the project?

   a) from b) about c) over

2. What are your plans .... expanding?

   a) for b) to c) under

3. I can't take any call .... the moment.

   a) in b) at c) until

4. I'm afraid I have to be .... now. I'll call you again later, OK?

   a) away b) over c) off

5. Winson Plc have based their marketing strategies .... our ideas.

   a) on b) by c) onto

▶ Siehe Grammatikteil: Verhältniswörter, Seite 116.

Wortschatz

Englisch	Deutsch
to take a call	ein Gespräch entgegennehmen
at the moment	zurzeit; augenblicklich
I'm afraid	es tut mir Leid; leider
Plc (= **public limited company**)	GmbH

Test

Lesen oder hören Sie den folgenden Text und beantworten Sie dann die nachstehende Frage:

It's a Mystery to Me

A couple of months ago, a most unfortunate thing happened. I was due to meet a business colleague from Munich, in London, outside the National Gallery in Trafalgar Square, before going on for dinner together. "Right, Wolfgang, see you on Friday at half seven," I said at the end of our telephone call. "OK, Steve, I'm looking forward to it!" replied Wolfgang. On the appointed day, I arrived at the National Gallery to find Wolfgang looking rather worried, and very cold (it was, after all, November). "Where have you been?" he asked, "I've been waiting for you for an hour!" What a misunderstanding! Poor Wolfgang!

What was the misunderstanding?

....

....

....

Englisch	Deutsch
mystery	Rätsel
to happen	geschehen; passieren
to be due to do sth.	etwas tun sollen
Munich	München
outside	draußen
to reply	erwidern
appointed	verabredet; festgelegt
worried	besorgt
misunderstanding	Missverständnis
poor	arm

Unit 6: Contracting

Lesen (und hören) Sie den folgenden Dialog:

Ian Ryden: Jonathan! How are you?
Jonathan Stacey: Fine, fine! I'll feel even better once the contracting has been sorted out!
Ian Ryden: Yes, that's one of the things I wanted to enquire about, actually ... Have the contracts been drawn up yet?
Jonathan Stacey: Not really. They're only in draft form at the moment.
Ian Ryden: How long will it take, do you suppose?
Jonathan Stacey: They'll be ready for the meeting in Manchester.
Ian Ryden: That reminds me, could your secretary book me a flight and some hotel accommodation? It would save me a lot of bother.
Jonathan Stacey: Of course. I'll put you through to her now, if you like.
Ian Ryden: Yes, please. Thanks a lot, Jonathan. Bye.
Jonathan Stacey: Goodbye for now, Ian.

A moment or two later ...

Secretary: Hello, Mr Ryden. Could you give me the details, please?
Ian Ryden: Yes, of course. I need a return flight from London Gatwick to Manchester on the 24th of April returning on the 26th of April and two nights' hotel accommodation.
Secretary: That shouldn't be a problem. I'll fax you the confirmation.
Ian Ryden: Thanks, I'd appreciate that. Goodbye.
Secretary: Goodbye, Mr Ryden.

Wortschatz

Englisch	Deutsch
contracting	Verträge abschließen
to sort out	klären; *auch:* aussortieren
actually	eigentlich
to draw up a contract	einen Vertrag aufsetzen

draft form	Entwurf
to take	dauern
to suppose	annehmen
That reminds me …	Dabei fällt mir ein …
(return) flight	(Hin- und Rück-)Flug
accommodation	Unterkunft
to save	sparen
bother	Ärger
confirmation	Bestätigung
to appreciate	schätzen
I'd appreciate that	Das wäre sehr nett von Ihnen.

A Ergänzen Sie im folgenden Dialog die Worte von Jonathan Stacey und der Sekretärin:

Ian Ryden: Jonathan! How are you?

Jonathan Stacey: ....

....

Ian Ryden: Yes, that's one of the things I wanted to enquire about, actually … Have the contracts been drawn up yet?

Jonathan Stacey: ....

....

Ian Ryden: How long will it take, do you suppose?

Jonathan Stacey: ....

Ian Ryden: That reminds me, could your secretary book me a flight and some hotel accommodation? It would save me a lot of bother.

Jonathan Stacey: ....

....

Ian Ryden: Yes, please. Thanks a lot, Jonathan. Bye.

Jonathan Stacey: ....

A moment or two later …

Secretary: ....

Ian Ryden: Yes, of course I need a return flight from London Gatwick to Manchester on the 24th of April returning on the 26th of April and two nights' hotel accommodation.

Secretary: ....

Ian Ryden: Thanks, I'd appreciate that. Goodbye.

Secretary: ....

Vergleichen Sie Ihre Antworten mit dem Originaltext.

- Hören Sie nun den Übungsdialog Abschnitt für Abschnitt an und sprechen Sie den jeweils gehörten Abschnitt nach.
- Hören Sie den Übungsdialog noch einmal an (nur Ian Ryden) und übernehmen Sie die Rolle von Jonathan Stacey und der Sekretärin.

B Ergänzen Sie im folgenden Dialog die Worte von Ian Ryden:

Ian Ryden: ....

Jonathan Stacey: Fine, fine! I'll feel even better once the contracting has been sorted out!

Ian Ryden: ....

....

....

Jonathan Stacey: Not really. They're only in draft form at the moment.

Ian Ryden: ....

Jonathan Stacey: They'll be ready for the meeting in Manchester.

Ian Ryden: ....

....

....

Jonathan Stacey: Of course. I'll put you through to her now, if you like.

Ian Ryden: ....

Jonathan Stacey: Goodbye for now, Ian.

A moment or two later …

Secretary: Hello, Mr Ryden. Could you give me the details, please?

Ian Ryden: ....

....

....

Secretary: That shouldn't be a problem. I'll fax you the confirmation.

Ian Ryden: ....

Secretary: Goodbye, Mr Ryden.

Vergleichen Sie Ihre Antworten mit dem Originaltext.

- Hören Sie den Übungsdialog ein drittes Mal an (nur Jonathan Stacey und die Sekretärin) und übernehmen Sie die Rolle von Ian Ryden.

Versuchen Sie, den Dialog zu ergänzen, ohne sich die Originaltexte anzuschauen. Und – ganz wichtig: Benutzen Sie Ihr Improvisationstalent!

Telephone Numbers

In English, telephone numbers are normally spoken as separate digits; so it would be usual to say: "six-three-nine-four-eight-seven-two" for 639 4872 (rather than "six hundred and thirty-nine four thousand eight hundred and seventy-two")! The word "double" is often used when two digits are the same, for example "double five", and "oh" is used for 0 (Americans say "zero"). Practise saying your own phone number in English now!

Englisch	Deutsch
normally	normalerweise
separate	einzelne(r)
digit	Ziffer; Bestandteil
rather than	eher als

Übung 1

Übersetzen Sie die folgenden Sätze ins Englische und benutzen Sie dabei jeweils ein **modales Hilfsverb** *(can/could/may/might/must/need/shall/should/will/would)* (→ Unit 1).

1. Was kann ich für Sie tun?

   ………………………………………………………………

2. Ich möchte Frau Waterson sprechen.

   ………………………………………………………………

3. Könnten Sie das bitte buchstabieren?

   ………………………………………………………………

4. Ich muss dringend mit Sarah Ward sprechen.

   ………………………………………………………………

5. Soll ich das aufschreiben?

   ………………………………………………………………

▶ Siehe Grammatikteil: modale Hilfsverben, Seite 115.

How You Talk is How You Feel

Although your counterpart on the telephone cannot actually see you in person, it is important to imagine that he or she can. The very fact that you cannot be seen lends great significance to your voice and to the way you speak. Sit up straight, but relaxed, and rest assured that your voice will sound relaxed, yet incisive. Smile when you speak – a smile can always be "heard" at the other end of the phone.

Wortschatz

Englisch	Deutsch
counterpart	Gegenstück; *hier:* Gesprächspartner(in *f*)
to imagine	sich vorstellen
to lend	verleihen
significance	Wichtigkeit

straight	gerade
rest assured	seien Sie versichert
incisive	treffend; präzise; *auch:* scharfsinnig
to smile	lächeln

Departments

Departments	**responsible for:**
Accounts	auditing accounts
Administration	managing company affairs
Advertising	publicity and promotion
Customer Service(s)	client and customer requirements
Finance	company financing
Marketing	commodity provision
Purchasing	product acquisition
Personnel	company employees
Sales	product selling

Englisch	Deutsch
department	Abteilung
Accounts	Buchhaltung
to audit	prüfen
Administration	Verwaltung
affair	Angelegenheit
Advertising	Werbeabteilung
promotion	Werbung
Customer Service(s)	Kundendienstabteilung
Finance	Finanzabteilung
Marketing	Marketingabteilung
commodity	Ware
provision	Beschaffung
Purchasing	Einkauf(sabteilung)
acquisition	Anschaffung
Personnel	Personal(abteilung)
employee	Angestellte(r)
Sales	Verkaufsabteilung

Übung 2

Benutzen Sie ein **Frageanhängsel** *(... are they?/... can't we?)*, um die folgenden Sätze zu vervollständigen (→ Unit 10).

1. Mr Worthington's line is still engaged, ... ?
2. You'd like to hold, ... ?
3. We must decide by Monday, ... ?
4. Your company employs three full-time advisers, ... ?
5. Sonia and Judy have received the agenda for the meeting, ... ?
6. It can't be true about the takeover bid, ... ?
7. Dan! You aren't really leaving the company, ... ?
8. Those strategies won't work in practice, ... ?
9. The figures don't reflect the actual position, ... ?
10. Mrs Foulds didn't fill in our questionnaire, ... ?

▶ Siehe Grammatikteil: Frageanhängsel, Seite 119.

Wortschatz

Englisch	**Deutsch**
to employ	anstellen; beschäftigen
agenda	Tagesordnung
takeover	Übernahme
figure	Zahl; Statistik
bid	Versuch
to reflect	widerspiegeln
questionnaire	Fragebogen

E-Mail

Übersetzen Sie die folgende E-Mail ins Englische:

Liebe Maggie,

hier sind die Details für die Reise nach New York:

Ich brauche einen Flug am Montag, dem 14. März, von Hamburg, der in New York am selben Tag ankommt. Ich bleibe bis Freitag in New York; bitte buchen Sie vier Nächte Hotelunterkunft und den Retourflug am Freitag, dem 18. März, von New York nach Hamburg.

Vielen Dank

Mike

Codes and Numbers

area code	Gebietsvorwahlnummer
country code	Landesvorwahlnummer
extension number	Durchwahlnummer
home number	Privatnummer
office number	Büronummer
postal code	Postleitzahl (UK)
work number	Geschäftsnummer
ZIP code (= Zone Improvement Plan)	Postleitzahl (US)

Übung 4

Setzen Sie die **Eigenschaftswörter** *(old/good/interesting)* unten in die **2. Steigerungsform** *(oldest/best/most interesting)*.

1. This project will be our (successful) .... one yet!
2. The annual trade fair in Birmingham is the (good) .... of its kind.
3. Britstone Brothers is the (old) .... firm dealing in these matters and the one with the (much) .... experience.
4. Your tactics are certainly the (interesting) .... I've ever heard, Clive!
5. Ms Danford's ideas go (far) .... in meeting our requirements.
6. We have to be the (fast) .... in the race towards quality commodity acquisition.
7. The (early) .... we can begin with the project is February.
8. Our basic strategies were, of course, (significant) .... in determining the direction we eventually took.
9. Their marketing department is the (efficient) .... one I have come across.
10. That's not the (bad) .... suggestion to be made!

Siehe Grammatikteil: Eigenschaftswörter, Seite 119.

Wortschatz

Englisch	Deutsch
annual	jährlich
ever	je(mals)
requirement	Bedürfnis
towards	auf … zu

significant	bedeutend; wichtig
to determine	bestimmen
eventually	schließlich
efficient	leistungsfähig
to come across sth.	treffen auf etwas

Wählen Sie das richtige Wort aus, um den unten stehenden Text zu ergänzen:

"Hello, Jennifer. How's (time/air/life) .... ? Look, can I ask you a (present/favour/invitation) .... ? I (worried/passed/missed) .... that meeting last week on concept implementation – you couldn't give me your notes, (would/should/could) .... you? I'm (sure/glad/casual) .... I can read your handwriting – or was there a (mystery/handout/deadline) .... ? I'd really (reply/have/appreciate) .... your help in this and if there's anything I can do for you, just give me a (bell/watch/clock) .... !"

Englisch	Deutsch
present	Geschenk
favour	Gefallen
to give sb. a bell	jdn. anrufen

Unit 7: Discussing Projects

Lesen (und hören) Sie den folgenden Dialog:

Kim Nolan: Well, Neil, I never thought we'd get this far!
Neil Webster: Quite, quite! Four months' underway already!
Kim Nolan: How's everyone bearing up your end?
Neil Webster: Feeling the pressure, I think, but it's not too much to cope with, especially compared to the last project.
Kim Nolan: Yes, that was a nightmare … Anyway, what's your prognosis? Do you think we can finish according to schedule?
Neil Webster: Well, we may run a little over the deadline, but generally, I feel things are going well; the reports are coming in, the meetings are taking place as planned, and so on.
Kim Nolan: That's a relief. Total immersion on all sides by the sound of it!
Neil Webster: Yes, the best way of course!
Kim Nolan: Talking of reports, when is the next one due?
Neil Webster: End of next week. I'll fax you a copy.
Kim Nolan: Great. Well, I'm glad to hear all's going well. By the way, give my regards to your wife.
Neil Webster: Thank you, I will. I've got a caller on the other line, so I'd better be off.
Kim Nolan: No problem. Bye, Neil.
Neil Webster: Goodbye.

Wortschatz

Englisch	Deutsch
quite	genau
to be underway	im Gang sein
to bear up	sich halten
pressure	Druck
to cope with sth.	zurechtkommen mit etwas
compared to	verglichen mit
nightmare	Alptraum
prognosis	Voraussage

according to	zufolge; laut
according to schedule	planmäßig
to run over (a deadline)	(einen Termin) überziehen
That's a relief.	Mir fällt ein Stein vom Herzen.
immersion	Vertieftsein
by the sound of it	es hört sich so an; es klingt; offensichtlich
due	fällig
regards	Grüße

A Ergänzen Sie im folgenden Dialog die Äußerungen von Neil Webster:

Kim Nolan: Well, Neil, I never thought we'd get this far!

Neil Webster: ....

Kim Nolan: How's everyone bearing up your end?

Neil Webster: ....

....

....

Kim Nolan: Yes, that was a nightmare … Anyway, what's your prognosis? Do you think we can finish according to schedule?

Neil Webster: ....

....

....

....

Kim Nolan: That's a relief. Total immersion on all sides by the sound of it!

Neil Webster: ....

Kim Nolan: Talking of reports, when is the next one due?

Neil Webster: ....

Kim Nolan: Great. Well, I'm glad to hear all's going well. By the way, give my regards to your wife.

Neil Webster: ....

....

Kim Nolan: No problem. Bye, Neil.

Neil Webster: ....

Vergleichen Sie Ihre Antworten mit dem Originaltext.

- Hören Sie nun den Übungsdialog Abschnitt für Abschnitt an und sprechen Sie den jeweils gehörten Abschnitt nach.
- Hören Sie den Übungsdialog noch einmal an (nur Kim Nolan) und übernehmen Sie die Rolle von Neil Webster.

B Ergänzen Sie im folgenden Dialog die Äußerungen von Kim Nolan:

Kim Nolan: ....

Neil Webster: Quite, quite! Four months' underway already!

Kim Nolan: ....

Neil Webster: Feeling the pressure, I think, but it's not too much to cope with, especially compared to the last project.

Kim Nolan: ....

....

....

Neil Webster: Well, we may run a little over the deadline, but generally, I feel things are going well; the reports are coming in, the meetings are taking place as planned, and so on.

Kim Nolan: ....

....

Neil Webster: Yes, the best way of course!

Kim Nolan: ....

Neil Webster: End of next week. I'll fax you a copy.

Kim Nolan: ....

....

Neil Webster: Thank you, I will. I've got a caller on the other line, so I'd better be off.

Kim Nolan: ....

Neil Webster: Goodbye.

Vergleichen Sie Ihre Antworten mit dem Originaltext.

- Hören Sie den Übungsdialog ein drittes Mal an (nur Neil Webster) und übernehmen Sie die Rolle von Kim Nolan.

Versuchen Sie, den Dialog zu ergänzen, ohne sich die Originaltexte anzuschauen. Es muss dabei keine genaue Wiedergabe des Originals herauskommen! Benutzen Sie Ihr Improvisationstalent!

Calls in the USA

The USA is the busiest country in the world when it comes to telephoning. It is the country where most calls are made; the figure stands at approximately 580 billion calls a year.

Englisch	Deutsch
world	Welt
figure	Zahl; Statistik
approximately (approx.)	ungefähr
billion	Milliarde

Übung 1

Übertragen Sie die folgenden Sätze in die **Verlaufsform des Imperfekts** *(I was writing/they were looking).*

1. I (type) .... still .... the report when Mr Brown asked for it, so I had to request more time to finish it.

2. The partners (discuss) .... the new deal when the phone rang and the client cancelled it.

3. Tracey (design) .... the graphics while Sid (write) .... the new programme.

4. You (talk) .... on the phone all morning yesterday!

5. The computers (not function) .... properly this afternoon, so we couldn't check the figures.

6. Ms Boreham (not write up) .... the minutes when I looked into the office this morning.

7. .... you (draw up) .... the contracts during lunch yesterday?

8. .... Kevin (brief) .... the new staff just now?

9. Who .... you (talk to) .... on the other line when I called?

10. What .... Alice (do) .... while I (entertain) .... the new clients?

Siehe Grammatikteil: Verlaufsform des Imperfekts, Seite 120.

Englisch	Deutsch
to request	bitten; ersuchen
deal	Geschäft; Handel
to cancel	rückgängig machen; streichen
properly	korrekt; richtig
minutes	Protokoll
to brief	instruieren
to entertain	unterhalten

How to Deal with an Angry Customer

The golden rule is: the customer is always right. When a distraught or dissatisfied customer comes on the line, allow him or her to voice their complaint, then apologise for the situation. Show sympathy, then offer to put things right. After all, the customer is giving you a chance to find a solution to the problem; courteously doing so enhances your (or your company's) reputation.

Englisch	Deutsch
golden rule	goldene Regel
the customer is always right	*etwa:* der Kunde ist König
distraught	verzweifelt; außer sich
dissatisfied	unzufrieden
to voice	zum Ausdruck bringen
complaint	Beschwerde; Klage
to apologise	sich entschuldigen
sympathy	Mitgefühl; Mitleid
after all	schließlich
courteously	höflich
to enhance	erhöhen

Abbreviations

E-mail	electronic mail
FAX	facsimile electronic transceiving equipment
GMT	Greenwich Mean (or: Meridian) Time
ISD	international subscriber dialling

Wortschatz

Englisch	Deutsch
to transceive	senden und empfangen
equipment	Ausrüstung
Greenwich Mean (*or:* Meridian) Time	Greenwicher Zeit; Westeuropäische Zeit
subscriber	Abonnent(in *f*)

Übung 2

Bilden Sie aus den folgenden Sätze **Fragen** *(Did you return his call?/Have you spoken to her?)*. Behalten Sie dabei stets die gleiche Zeitform bei (→ Unit 1, 3 und 8).

1. Jill Norman is holding the first meeting in two weeks' time.

   ....?

2. They exhibit their new products at every trade fair.

   ....?

3. Rosemary will complete the task in time.

   ....?

4. We are going to draw up the contracts next week.

   ....?

5. Messrs Trowbridge and Sons dealt with the marketing.

   ....?

6. His phone was engaged the whole morning.

   ....?

7. Oliver has appointed two more directors.

....?

8. They were designing new layouts all day yesterday.

....?

9. You can outline the regulations to the new members of staff, Bill.

....?

10. There isn't enough background information.

....?

Siehe Grammatikteil: Fragen, Seite 115f.

Wortschatz

Englisch	**Deutsch**
to retain	(bei)behalten
to exhibit	ausstellen
task	Aufgabe
to appoint	einstellen
regulation	Vorschrift

Übung 3

Telephone Conversation

Hören oder lesen Sie den folgenden Telefondialog und beantworten Sie dann die Fragen unten mit »richtig« oder »falsch«.

Switchboard: Greenwood Enterprises, can I help you?
Caller: Hello, could I speak to Mrs Bell, please?
Switchboard: Who's calling, please?
Caller: My name's Gray.
Switchboard: Thank you, Mr Gray, one moment please. (*Pause*) I'm putting you through now.
Caller: Thank you very much.
Mrs Bell: Hello, Mr Gray. What can I do for you?
Caller: I'm a reporter for a local newspaper, the Daily News, and I was wondering if you could give me any information about your exhibition stand at this year's trade fair.

Mrs Bell:	I'm sorry, that's confidential information at present.
Caller:	When will you be able to release details?
Mrs Bell:	Our press officer will take care of that side of things as soon as the time is right.
Caller:	Well, perhaps I'll call back next week.
Mrs Bell:	That won't be necessary, we'll call you.
Caller:	Well, OK, thank you.
Mrs Bell:	Thank you, goodbye.

1. The caller would like to speak to Mrs Bell. ☐
2. The caller gives his first name. ☐
3. Mrs Bell's line is busy. ☐
4. The caller works as a newsreader for a local radio station. ☐
5. The caller would like information regarding Greenwood Enterprises' exhibition stand. ☐
6. Mrs Bell gives the caller the information he requires. ☐
7. Mrs Bell transfers the caller to the press officer. ☐
8. The press officer will probably phone the caller back. ☐

Wortschatz

Englisch	**Deutsch**
wonder	sich fragen
confidential	vertraulich
to release	veröffentlichen
to take care of sth.	sich um etwas kümmern
necessary	nötig

Company Employees

accountant	Buchhalter(in *f*)
administrative assistant	Verwaltungsassistent(in *f*)
managing director	leitende(r) Direktor(in *f*); Geschäftsführer(in *f*)
office clerk	Büroangestellte(r)
personal assistant	Direktionsassistent(in *f*)
personnel manager	Personalleiter(in *f*)
receptionist	Empfangssekretär(in *f*)
sales director/manager	Verkaufsleiter(in *f*)
secretary	(Betriebs-)Sekretär(in *f*)
typist	Schreibkraft
vice chairman	Vizepräsident(in *f*)

Übertragen Sie die folgenden Sätze in die **indirekte Rede** *(He said that they were away/She asked if she could phone back later)*.

1. "David Saunders is extremely busy."

   She said that ....

   ....

2. "Georgina and Rick can't make it to the meeting."

   He told his boss that ....

   ....

3. "We aren't bringing out a new edition yet."

   They informed the staff that ....

   ....

4. "Margaret doesn't have time to attend all the meetings."

   Tim told us that ....

   ....

5. “I will call them back as soon as possible.”

Mandy said that ....

....

6. “Simon Kirk and James Walker are going to give a presentation.”

Mrs Blake mentioned that ....

....

7. “Does your assistant book your flights for you?”

Ian asked me if ....

....

8. “Can Mr Charlton give me a ring when he has time?”

The client wanted to know if ....

....

Siehe Grammatikteil: indirekte Rede, Seite 120.

Wortschatz

Englisch	**Deutsch**
to make it to the (meeting)	es schaffen, zum (Treffen) zu kommen
edition	Auflage
to attend (a meeting)	an (einem Treffen) teilnehmen; besuchen
presentation	Vortrag
to mention	erwähnen

Finden Sie ein **Synonym** *(she booked a flight = she reserved a flight)* für die Wörter in Schrägschrift. Behalten Sie dabei stets die gleiche Form bei:

1. I'm *putting you through* now. ....
2. We *are sorry* for the delay. ....
3. Miss Irvine's line is *busy* at present. ....
4. Thank you for *calling*. ....
5. The *yearly* meeting is always held in May. ....
6. Preparations for the trade fair are now *well underway*. ....
7. Everything is going according to *plan*. ....
8. Who are they going to *give the job to?* ....

Unit 8: Project Extending

Lesen (und hören) Sie den folgenden Dialog:

Geoffrey Allan: Hello, Anita!
Anita Morris: Hello, Geoff. Well, we've done it at last!
Geoffrey Allan: I know. Marvellous feeling, isn't it?
Anita Morris: I never thought we'd manage it in time. I'm looking forward to the convention now. Aren't you?
Geoffrey Allan: Oh yes. At times I thought we were cutting things a little fine …
Anita Morris: Yes, in fact, we only took delivery of the pamphlets from the printer yesterday. The girls are just counting and sorting them now, actually.
Geoffrey Allan: Things have turned out well, really, considering that the convention is scheduled two weeks earlier than usual this year.
Anita Morris: All we'll have to do then is collate the convention reports and attach them as appendix material – and hey presto!
Geoffrey Allan: And then we'll really be able to celebrate!
Anita Morris: Yes, I suppose we will.
Geoffrey Allan: Right, see you at the convention, then.
Anita Morris: Of course. Thanks for ringing, Geoff.
Geoffrey Allan: My pleasure. Goodbye.
Anita Morris: Bye.

Englisch	Deutsch
at last	endlich
marvellous	wunderbar
to manage	schaffen
at times	manchmal
to cut things fine	knapp sein/werden
to take delivery of sth.	etwas in Empfang nehmen
pamphlet	Broschüre
printer	Drucker
to count	zählen
to turn out	sich ergeben
considering	wenn man bedenkt
to collate	zusammentragen
to attach	beiheften
appendix (pl. appendices)	Anhang
Hey presto!	Hokuspokus!
to celebrate	feiern

A Ergänzen Sie im folgenden Dialog die Worte von Anita Morris:

Geoffrey Allan: Hello, Anita!

Anita Morris: ....

Geoffrey Allan: I know. Marvellous feeling, isn't it?

Anita Morris: ....

....

Geoffrey Allan: Oh yes. At times I thought we were cutting things a little fine …

Anita Morris: ....

....

....

Geoffrey Allan: Things have turned out well, really, considering that the convention is scheduled two weeks earlier than usual this year.

Anita Morris: ....

....

....

Geoffrey Allan: And then we'll really be able to celebrate!

Anita Morris: ....

Geoffrey Allan: Right, see you at the convention, then.

Anita Morris: ....

Geoffrey Allan: My pleasure. Goodbye.

Anita Morris: ....

Vergleichen Sie Ihre Antworten mit dem Originaltext.

- Hören Sie nun den Übungsdialog Abschnitt für Abschnitt an und sprechen Sie den jeweils gehörten Abschnitt nach.
- Hören Sie sich den Übungsdialog noch einmal an (nur Geoffrey Allan) und übernehmen Sie die Rolle von Anita Morris.

B Setzen Sie im folgenden Dialog die Worte von Geoffrey Allan ein:

Geoffrey Allan: ....

Anita Morris: Hello, Geoff. Well, we've done it at last!

Geoffrey Allan: ....

Anita Morris: I never thought we'd manage it in time. I'm looking forward to the convention now. Aren't you?

Geoffrey Allan: ....

....

Anita Morris: Yes, in fact we only took delivery of the pamphlets from the printer yesterday. The girls are just counting and sorting them now, actually.

Geoffrey Allan: ....

....

....

Anita Morris: All we'll have to do then is collate the convention reports and attach them as appendix material – and hey presto!

Geoffrey Allan: ....

Anita Morris: Yes, I suppose we will.

Geoffrey Allan: ....

Anita Morris: Of course. Thanks for ringing, Geoff.

Geoffrey Allan: ....

Anita Morris: Bye.

Vergleichen Sie Ihre Antworten mit dem Originaltext.

- Hören Sie den Übungsdialog ein drittes Mal an (nur Anita Morris) und übernehmen Sie die Rolle von Geoffrey Allan.

Versuchen Sie, den Dialog zu ergänzen, ohne auf die Originaltexte zu schauen. Dabei muss es sich nicht um eine genaue Wiedergabe des Originals handeln. Benutzen Sie Ihr Improvisationstalent!

Reverse(d) Charge Calls

A call that is paid for by the person who receives it is a "reverse(d) charge call" (US: "collect call").

Englisch	Deutsch
paid (for)	bezahlt
to receive	empfangen; erhalten
reverse(d) charge call (UK)	R-Gespräch
collect call (US)	R-Gespräch

Übung 1

Finden Sie für die unten stehende Sätze und Fragen in der **Verlaufsform des Perfekts** die jeweils richtige Erwiderung *(I have been writing/he has been looking)*:

1. I've been trying to get through all morning!
2. How long have you been waiting, Vicky?
3. I'm sorry I'm late – what have you all been discussing?
4. How often have you been holding the meetings?
5. Mr Hinton has been dealing with your complaint, sir.

Lösung:

1	
2	
3	
4	
5	

a) Whether or not to take on more business.
b) Good. Please inform me immediately of the outcome.
c) Oh, about five minutes.
d) I'm sorry, the lines have been very busy.
e) Approximately once a month.

▶ Siehe Grammatikteil: Verlaufsform des Perfekts, Seite 120.

Wortschatz

Englisch	Deutsch
to get through	durchkommen
whether	ob
to take on	annehmen
approximately (approx.)	ungefähr

Bad Connections

In today's hi-tech world of telecommunications, lines do occasionally get crossed – in extreme cases often with hilarious results. Problems range from faint lines ("I can hardly hear you") through interference on the line ("There's a terrible noise on the line"), to party lines, with two or more unrelated speakers on the same line at the same time, with nothing more in common than a faulty connection.

Wortschatz

Englisch	Deutsch
hi-tech (= high technology)	hochtechnologisch
occasionally	gelegentlich
to get a crossed line	jdn. in der Leitung haben
hilarious	komisch; lustig
to range from … through … to	gehen von … über/ … bis
faint	entfernt
hardly	kaum
interference	Störung
noise	Lärm
party line	Gemeinschaftsanschluss
unrelated	ohne Beziehung zueinander
to have sth. in common	etwas miteinander gemein haben
faulty	defekt

Telephone Conferences

An increasingly popular form of business communication is the "telephone conference", which enables the head office of a company to keep in touch with its subsidiaries by setting up a multi-participant conversation – in effect, a business "party line".

Wortschatz

Englisch	Deutsch
increasingly	zunehmend
popular	beliebt
to enable	ermöglichen
to keep in touch	auf dem Laufenden bleiben; in Kontakt bleiben
subsidiary (company)	Tochtergesellschaft
to set up	vereinbaren; arrangieren
multi-participant	mit mehreren Teilnehmern
in effect	in Wirklichkeit; praktisch

Übung 2

Wählen Sie das passende **Umstandswort** *(slowly/immediately/fast)* aus, um die Sätze zu vervollständigen:

1. Could I use your phone (quick/quickly), Sandra?
2. I'd like to speak to Dr Wheeler (personal/personally), please.
3. Could you (possibly/possible) call me back later?
4. Did you understand our advertisement (correctly/correct), madam?
5. Sue, you've been working too (hard/hardly). Take it easy!
6. I can't hear you. Speak a bit more (loudly/loud), sir.
7. It's a bad line; I can't hear you very (good/well).
8. We can (officially/official) give you the estimate in about a month's time.
9. Let me have the expenditure figures for November (immediate/immediately), please.
10. Thank you for ringing back so (prompt/promptly).

► Siehe Grammatikteil: Umstandswörter, Seite 120 f.

Wortschatz

Englisch	**Deutsch**
advertisement	Werbung; Reklame; Anzeige
estimate	Kostenvoranschlag; Schätzung
expenditure	Ausgaben
prompt	pünktlich; schnell

Übung 3

Memo

You would like to set up a telephone conference with the press officers of your subsidiary companies. Write a memo to the switchboard operator, detailing the date and time, and asking her to set up the conference.

Time Differences

Before you make an international call, remember that the time may differ in the country you are phoning!
For example:
Munich is one hour ahead of London.
New York is six hours behind Munich.
Manchester is one hour behind Hamburg.
Tokyo is eight hours ahead of Frankfurt.

Wortschatz

Englisch	Deutsch
time difference	Zeitunterschied
to differ	sich unterscheiden
ahead	um … voraus
behind	um … hinterher

Übung 4

Setzen Sie die alternative Form der **Uhrzeit** *(ten to seven in the morning = 6.50 a.m.)* ein, um die Sätze zu vervollständigen (→ Unit 5).

1. It's twenty-five past four in the afternoon. That means it's:

   ....

2. It's eight o'clock in the morning. That means it's:

   ....

3. It's ten minutes past seven in the evening. That means it's:

   ....

4. It's twenty-five to twelve in the morning. That means it's:

   ....

5. It's half past three in the afternoon. That means it's:

   ....

6. It's twenty to eleven at night. That means it's:

   ....

7. It's quarter past nine in the morning. That means it's:

   ....

8. It's eight o'clock in the evening. That means it's:

   ....

9. It's five past two in the afternoon. That means it's:

   ....

10. It's quarter to three in the morning. That means it's:

    ....

▶ Siehe wichtige Grundbegriffe: Uhrzeit, Seite 9.

Setzen Sie in das folgende Telefongespräch die richtigen **Fragewörter** ein (→ Unit 1, 3 und 7):

"Hello, Clive Norman calling from Hanover. Lucy, ... are you? Fine, I hope. ....'s the weather like over in Washington? It's been pouring down for days here! I've got a few questions to ask you regarding the response to our questionnaire. Firstly, ... were actually sent back? About five hundred? Not bad at all! .... have you appointed to analyse them? Jean Hoyle? Great! .... will she be based? At Head Office? Oh, good, it'll be easier to contact her there. Have you got any idea .... she'll need? A month? .... so long? That's too long. Tell her three weeks at the most! Let me know what she says. .... are you coming over to Europe? Soon? Make it sooner! OK. Keep in touch. Bye for now, Lucy."

Siehe Grammatikteil: Fragen, Seite 115.

Wortschatz

Englisch	Deutsch
to pour down	in Strömen gießen
to appoint	einstellen
soon	bald
Keep in touch!	Lass wieder mal von dir hören!

Unit 9: Closing Down

Lesen (und hören) Sie den folgenden Dialog:

Derek: Hello, Tony. How are you feeling, now that the pressure's off?

Tony: Well, it's a bit of an anticlimax, really! We're winding down now, which is what I wanted to talk to you about.

Derek: Fire away!

Tony: Well, there are several matters to be dealt with: debriefing the team; releasing the extra staff we took on at the commencement of the project; setting up a circulation survey, to name but a few.

Derek: I see … A project in itself, actually!

Tony: Quite. Would you be prepared to deal with the staff? That would leave me free to handle the circulation angle; I'd like to find out what kind of exposure we have achieved.

Derek: Sure, leave the staff to me. On the whole, do you think we've been successful?

Tony: It's hard to say right now … An exhibition is theoretically a good source of potential customers, but in practice, who knows?

Derek: Indeed. Anyway, I'll get back to you about the staff.

Tony: Thanks, Derek. Speak to you soon. Bye.

Derek: Goodbye.

Englisch	Deutsch
anticlimax	Enttäuschung
to wind down	zurückschrauben
to fire away	losschießen
matter	Angelegenheit
to debrief sb.	den Einsatz (anschließend) besprechen mit jdm.
to release	entlassen
circulation	Auflage
survey	Umfrage
angle	Standpunkt
exposure	Publicity
to achieve	erreichen
on the whole	im Ganzen gesehen
source	Quelle
indeed	allerdings

A Setzen Sie in den folgenden Dialog die Worte von Tony ein:

Derek: Hello, Tony. How are you feeling, now that the pressure's off?

Tony: ....

....

....

Derek: Fire away!

Tony: ....

....

....

....

Derek: I see … A project in itself, actually!

Tony: ....

....

....

....

Derek: Sure, leave the staff to me. On the whole, do you think we've been successful?

Tony: ....

....

....

Derek: Indeed. Anyway, I'll get back to you about the staff.

Tony: ....

Derek: Goodbye.

Vergleichen Sie Ihre Antworten mit dem Originaltext.

- Hören Sie nun den Übungsdialog Abschnitt für Abschnitt an und sprechen Sie den jeweils gehörten Abschnitt nach.
- Hören Sie den Übungsdialog noch einmal an (nur Derek) und übernehmen Sie die Rolle von Tony.

B Ergänzen Sie im folgenden Dialog die Worte von Derek:

Derek: ....

....

Tony: Well, it's a bit of an anticlimax, really! We're winding down now, which is what I wanted to talk to you about.

Derek: ....

Tony: Well, there are several matters to be dealt with: debriefing the team; releasing the extra staff we took on at the commencement of the project; setting up a circulation survey, to name but a few.

Derek: ....

Tony: Quite. Would you be prepared to deal with the staff? That would leave me free to handle the circulation angle; I'd like to find out what kind of exposure we have achieved.

Derek: ....

....

Tony: It's hard to say right now ... An exhibition is theoretically a good source of potential customers, but in practice, who knows?

Derek: ....

....

Tony: Thanks, Derek. Speak to you soon. Bye.

Derek: ....

Vergleichen Sie Ihre Antworten mit dem Originaltext.

- Hören Sie den Übungsdialog (nur Tony) ein drittes Mal an und übernehmen Sie die Rolle von Derek.

Versuchen Sie, den Dialog zu ergänzen, ohne auf die Originaltexte zu schauen. Ihr Improvisationstalent ist gefragt!

Calls in the UK

There are approximately 30 million telephones in the UK and more than 60 million phone calls are made every day.

Übung 1

Übersetzen Sie die folgenden Sätze ins Englische und benutzen Sie dabei das Verb **would**.

1. Wären Sie bereit, mit unseren Partnern zu sprechen?

   ....

2. Würden Sie das bitte buchstabieren?

   ....

3. Ich möchte lieber zuerst ins Büro gehen.

....

4. Wir hätten gern ein paar Informationen über die nächste Sitzung.

....

5. Ich würde Herrn Edwards gern geschäftlich sprechen.

....

6. Es wäre eine gute Idee, Ihre Vorschläge mit uns zu besprechen.

....

7. Möchten Sie eine Nachricht hinterlassen?

....

8. Ich hätte gern seine Durchwahlnummer.

....

Siehe Grammatikteil: *would*, Seite 121.

No Time to Talk! What do you do if the phone rings just as you are on your way out? It is, of course, awkward if you have to cut a conversation short, but it is, at times, unavoidable. Above all, telephone manners should be retained; all it takes is a quiet apology, accompanied by the reason you are pressed for time, and a promise to call back at a more convenient time.

Englisch	Deutsch
awkward	ungünstig
unavoidable	unvermeidlich
to retain	(bei)behalten
apology	Entschuldigung
accompanied	begleitet
reason	Grund
to be pressed for time	unter Termindruck stehen
promise	Versprechen
convenient	günstig; passend

Telemessages

The traditional telegram has now been renamed the "telemessage". The service remains unchanged: you simply phone the operator, give him or her your message, and the message is delivered by post the following day.

Englisch	Deutsch
traditional	traditionell
to rename	umbenennen
simply	einfach
to deliver	liefern

Übung 2

Benutzen Sie die richtige Form von "be", um die folgenden Sätze in die **Passivform** zu übertragen *(the letters were written/the matter was looked into).*

1. The AGM .... held in Bournemouth last year.
2. A review of company profits will .... carried out next month.
3. The contract has .... drawn up already, Andy.
4. Your flight and hotel room .... reserved, Ms Walker.
5. How many questionnaires have .... filled in?
6. Hundreds of calls .... made every week.
7. Our departments ....n't debriefed after last month's completion.
8. I think I .... cut off!
9. I'm sorry but your call can't .... put through.
10. When .... the matter dealt with and by whom?

Siehe Grammatikteil: Passiv, Seite 121.

Wortschatz

Englisch	Deutsch
AGM (= Annual General Meeting)	jährliche Hauptversammlung
review	Rückblick; Überblick
to debrief sb.	den Einsatz (anschließend) besprechen mit
to be cut off	unterbrochen werden

Telephone Conversation

Hören oder lesen Sie den folgenden Dialog und entscheiden Sie, welcher der drei unten stehenden Texte richtig ist.

Mark: Hello, Alice, how's it going?
Alice: Fine – at last it's all over!
Mark: How long did the project take to complete?
Alice: Eight months, from the pilot meeting until the launch of the product.
Mark: And how often did you meet to discuss its progress?
Alice: We held monthly meetings.
Mark: So you were kept really busy!
Alice: Yes – there were two very important highlights. One was when we exhibited the prototype at the Newton Trade Show about four months into the project.
Mark: And the other?
Alice: The final exhibition of the product at the 20th Century Fair in Liverpool.
Mark: So, I expect you're ready for a holiday!
Alice: I certainly am!
Mark: Well, hope to see you around sometime.
Alice: Yes, see you, bye.

A The project took eight months to complete, there were eight meetings a month and the product was finally exhibited at the Newton Trade Show.

B The project took four months to complete, there were eight meetings and the product was then exhibited at the 20th Century Fair in Liverpool.

C The project took eight months to complete, there was a meeting once a month and the product was exhibited at the Newton Trade Show after four months.

Alexander Graham Bell

The telephone is more than 100 years old; it was invented by Scottish-born Alexander Graham Bell (1847–1922) and was patented in 1876.

Wortschatz

Englisch	Deutsch
more than	mehr als
to invent	erfinden
Scottish	schottisch
born	geboren
to patent	patentieren lassen

Übung 4

Benutzen Sie ein Zeitwort in der **Befehlsform** *(write/look)*, um die folgenden Sätze zu vervollständigen (→ Unit 3).

1. Please .... patient. The line will soon be free.
2. Don't .... in touch with him yet; the matter can wait until next week.
3. Ms Reed's line's engaged. .... again later.
4. .... Lindsay that the shareholders want to call a meeting.
5. .... with the matter as soon as you can, please.
6. Mr Dawson – .... me two nights' hotel accommodation for the AGM, please.
7. .... the staff about the company award, Sonia.
8. Please don't .... the summons.
9. Amanda – .... a telephone conference for next Monday, would you?
10. .... a note of their phone number in case you need it.

Siehe Grammatikteil: Befehlsform, Seite 117.

Wortschatz

Englisch	Deutsch
patient	geduldig
shareholder	Aktionär(in *f*)
award	Preis; Auszeichnung
summons	Aufruf; Aufforderung
in case	falls

Test

Wählen Sie den richtigen Zeitausdruck für die folgenden Sätze:

1. We're going to conclude the project by ....

   a) next year. b) last week. c) recently.

2. Presumably, the decision has been taken ....

   a) tomorrow. b) in July. c) already.

3. Was there a departmental meeting ....

   a) next week? b) yet? c) on Monday?

4. Is there a general consensus on the subject ....

   a) at the moment? b) in 1997? c) next Christmas?

5. Wilton Ltd were still in the process of liquidating ....

   a) now. b) two months ago. c) next week.

Wortschatz

Englisch	Deutsch
to conclude	abschließen
recently	kürzlich; vor kurzem
presumably	vermutlich
consensus	Übereinstimmung
to liquidate	auflösen

Unit 10: Recapitulating

Lesen (und hören) Sie den folgenden Dialog:

Carol Mitchell: Is that you, Sam?

Sam Bradley: Yes, hi, Carol!

Carol Mitchell: So – everything over and done with, at long last!

Sam Bradley: Yes, and such a resounding success!

Carol Mitchell: I hear there's been a lot of feedback …

Sam Bradley: Yes, and overwhelmingly positive; we've had numerous enquiries and several contracts have been agreed already.

Carol Mitchell: What about any of the giants?

Sam Bradley: Well, Pan Freightlines have expressed interest; we're hoping to set up talks soon.

Carol Mitchell: That's great! So, how long do you reckon the whole project took from start to finish?

Sam Bradley: From the inaugural meeting to the last survey analysis … eighteen months exactly. A little longer than anticipated, but we got there in the end!

Carol Mitchell: So it's time to start thinking about the next campaign!

Sam Bradley: Let me recover from this one first! Why don't we have lunch together next week?

Carol Mitchell: Good idea! What about Friday, one o'clock, at "Paprika"?

Sam Bradley: That's fine by me. I'm looking forward to it already.

Carol Mitchell: OK, see you then. Bye, Sam.

Sam Bradley: Goodbye, Carol.

Englisch	Deutsch
over and done with	fertig und vorbei
at long last	schließlich und endlich
resounding	gewaltig; durchschlagend
overwhelming(ly)	überwältigend; umwerfend
numerous	zahlreich
giant	Riese; Gigant
freightline(s)	Frachtfirma
to express	ausdrücken
to reckon	meinen; schätzen
inaugural	Eröffnungs-
anticipated	vorausgesehen; erwartet
campaign	Kampagne; Aktion
to recover	erholen

A Ergänzen Sie den folgenden Dialog mit den Worten von Sam Bradley:

Carol Mitchell: Is that you, Sam?

Sam Bradley: ....

Carol Mitchell: So – everything over and done with, at long last!

Sam Bradley: ....

Carol Mitchell: I hear there's been a lot of feedback …

Sam Bradley: ....

....

....

Carol Mitchell: What about any of the giants?

Sam Bradley: ....

....

Carol Mitchell: That's great! So, how long do you reckon the whole project took from start to finish?

Sam Bradley: ....

....

....

Carol Mitchell: So it's time to start thinking about the next campaign!

Sam Bradley: ....

....

Carol Mitchell: Good idea! What about Friday, one o'clock, at "Paprika"?

Sam Bradley: ....

....

Carol Mitchell: OK, see you then. Bye, Sam.

Sam Bradley: ....

Vergleichen Sie Ihre Antworten mit dem Originaltext.

- Hören Sie nun den Übungsdialog Abschnitt für Abschnitt an und sprechen Sie den jeweils gehörten Abschnitt nach.
- Hören Sie den Übungsdialog noch einmal an (nur Carol Mitchell) und übernehmen Sie die Rolle von Sam Bradley.

B Ergänzen Sie im folgenden Dialog die Worte von Carol Mitchell:

Carol Mitchell: ....
Sam Bradley: Yes, hi, Carol!

Carol Mitchell: ....
Sam Bradley: Yes, and such a resounding success!

Carol Mitchell: ....
Sam Bradley: Yes, and overwhelmingly positive; we've had numerous enquiries and several contracts have been agreed already.

Carol Mitchell: ....
Sam Bradley: Well, Pan Freightlines have expressed interest; we're hoping to set up talks soon.

Carol Mitchell: ....

....

Sam Bradley: From the inaugural meeting to the last survey analysis ... eighteen months exactly. A little longer than anticipated, but we got there in the end!

Carol Mitchell: ....

....

Sam Bradley: Let me recover from this one first! Why don't we have lunch together next week?

Carol Mitchell: ....

....

Sam Bradley: That's fine by me. I'm looking forward to it already.

Carol Mitchell: ....

Sam Bradley: Goodbye, Carol.

Vergleichen Sie Ihre Antworten mit dem Originaltext.

- Hören Sie den Übungsdialog ein drittes Mal an (nur Sam Bradley) und übernehmen Sie die Rolle von Carol Mitchell.

Versuchen Sie, den Dialog zu ergänzen, ohne auf die Originaltexte zu schauen. Denken Sie daran – es muss keine genaue Wiedergabe des Originals sein. Benutzen Sie Ihr Improvisationstalent!

Street Directions

- Go out of the station and turn left.
- Cross the road and take the second turning on the right.
- Go straight ahead until you come to some crossroads.
- Turn right and it's the large green building on the left.
- Go through the main door and take the lift to the third floor.
- The office is at the end of the corridor on the right.

Wortschatz

Englisch	Deutsch
street directions	Straßenangaben; Wegbeschreibungen
to turn	abbiegen
to cross	überqueren
turning	Abbiegung
straight ahead	geradeaus
crossroads	Straßenkreuzung
main door	Haupteingang
floor	Stockwerk; *auch:* Boden
corridor	Gang

Übung 1

Wählen Sie die richtige **Zeitform** und ergänzen Sie die folgenden Sätze (→ Unit 2 und 3).

1. The staff meeting .... place at the moment.

   a) will take **b)** is taking **c)** has taken

2. We .... the members of the team tomorrow morning.

   a) briefed **b)** have briefed **c)** are going to brief

3. I .... you through now, madam.

   a) will put **b)** was putting **c)** put

4. Our company normally .... a customer survey once a year.

   a) is doing **b)** is going to do **c)** does

▶ Siehe Grammatikteil: Gegenwarts- und Zukunftsformen, Seite 116 ff.

The British Telephone Box

If it becomes necessary to make a phone call from a public place, don't worry if you cannot find a *red* telephone box! Although many of the characteristic, red telephone boxes were sold off in the eighties and replaced by impersonal glass and chrome cabins in town and city centres, the observant visitor to Great Britain may spot one of the famous old British telephone boxes in a long-forgotten corner of an out-of-the-way village or tiny hamlet tucked away in the countryside!

Wortschatz

Englisch	Deutsch
to replace	ersetzen
observant	aufmerksam
visitor	Besucher
corner	Ecke
village	Dorf
tiny	winzig
hamlet	Weiler; kleines Dorf
tucked away	versteckt

Public Telephone Box Instructions

- Lift the receiver.
- Insert the correct money.
- Wait for the dialling tone.
- Dial the number you require.
- After the call, replace the receiver.

Wortschatz

Englisch	Deutsch
receiver	Hörer
to insert	einwerfen
dialling tone	Amtszeichen
to replace (the receiver)	auflegen (den Hörer)

Übung 2

Füllen Sie die Lücken in den Sätzen, indem Sie das **einfache Imperfekt** oder das **einfache Perfekt** (→ Unit 4) benutzen:

1. Alex (analyse) .... not .... the results of the survey yet.
2. We (have) .... not .... time to check the invoices last week.
3. I (send) .... you an e-mail yesterday.
4. The client (respond) .... to the suggestion already.
5. .... you (write up) .... that report on Friday?
6. .... the new members of staff (meet) .... the head of department yet?
7. Which country .... Ms Smythe never (be) .... to on business?
8. When .... you finally (complete) .... the report?

► Siehe Grammatikteil: einfaches Imperfekt und einfaches Perfekt, Seite 118.

Wortschatz

Englisch	Deutsch
survey	Umfrage
invoice	Rechnung
suggestion	Vorschlag
finally	endlich

Übung 3

Draft

You would like to telephone the managing directors of your subsidiary companies thanking them for their part in the completion of the project and congratulating them on their efforts. Write a draft of what you intend to say to them.

....

....

....

....

....

....

Antique Telephones

As technology races ahead, the antique value of telephones has increased dramatically. Ranging from the classic instruments from the Edwardian era to the Bakelite models of the 1930s, old telephones can fetch anything up to £1000 at auction today.

Wortschatz

Englisch	Deutsch
to race ahead	mit Riesenschritten vorangehen
value	Wert
instrument	Gerät
era	Epoche
to fetch	(ein)bringen
auction	Versteigerung

Übung 4

Wählen Sie das richtige **Frageanhängsel** (→ Unit 6) aus.

1. Get back to me about the survey, ... | 1 | |
2. The rooms have been reserved, ... | 2 | |
3. There wasn't much feedback, ... | 3 | |

Übung 4

4. Ms Wolfe has been dealing with the press,

....

5. We weren't doing very well this time last year,

....

6. They didn't inform the marketing department,

....

7. Sally, you could write up the minutes,

....

8. Simon won't miss the meeting, ...

9. We've gained quite a lot of new customers,

....

10. It's been a good year, ...

4	
5	
6	
7	
8	
9	
10	

a) hasn't it?
b) haven't we?
c) will he?
d) was there?
e) couldn't you?
f) were we?
g) would you?
h) did they?
i) hasn't she?
j) haven't they?

Siehe Grammatikteil: Frageanhängsel, Seite 119.

Schlusstest

Benutzen Sie ein **persönliches** oder **besitzanzeigendes Fürwort** oder ein **modales Hilfsverb**, ein **Fragewort**, ein **Verhältniswort**, ein Zeitwort in der richtigen **Zeitform**, ein **Bestimmungswort**, **some** oder **any**, eine **2. Steigerungsform** oder ein **Umstandswort**, um den folgenden Text zu ergänzen:

A Day to Remember!

.... few days ago, ... colleagues at the office played a (embarrassing) .... trick on me on what must be the (bad) .... day of my working life. I work for a small company which is a subsidiary of a giant national corporation. I'm a research coordinator and my job entails spending a lot .... time on the telephone, collating information and delegating. Anyway, as I entered the office, three of my workmates were (sit) .... there, looking very serious. I had to return a call from a group leader in one of the other companies, as a matter of urgency. I dialled the number they had noted down .... me and just had time to ask " .... may I help you?" when I was (greet) .... by a torrent of abuse. I had never heard such rudeness and felt my temper rising. I (begin) .... to give as good as I was getting, my voice getting louder and louder. I was red .... the face and shouting, pacing .... office and (wild) .... waving my free arm about. After .... minutes, I became aware that my three colleagues were laughing. And then it dawned on me; it was a trick telephone line with a prerecorded voice-over – one of those you .... dial to play a prank on a colleague. My colleagues had a good laugh at my expense .... day, and at my rage – and I am still (wait) .... to pay .... back – .... day now!

Englisch	Deutsch
embarrassing	peinlich
trick	Streich
corporation	(Handels-)Gesellschaft
to entail	erforderlich machen; darin bestehen
workmate	Arbeitskollegin
serious	ernst
urgency	Dringlichkeit
torrent of abuse	Schwall von Beschimpfungen
rudeness	Unverschämtheit; Grobheit
temper	Wut
to give as good as you get	es jdm. mit gleicher Münze heimzahlen
to pace	auf und ab gehen
to wave about	herumfuchteln
aware	bewusst
to laugh	lachen
to dawn on sb.	jdm. dämmern
to prerecord	vorher aufzeichnen
prank	Streich
at my expense	auf meine Kosten
rage	Wut

Kurzgrammatik

Persönliche und besitzanzeigende Fürwörter (→ Unit 1)

1 *Persönliche Fürwörter*

I/me/you/he/him/she/her/it/we/us/they/them sind persönliche Fürwörter und werden verwendet, um Hauptwörter zu ersetzen (z. B. The partners are in London = They are in London).

2 *Besitzanzeigende Fürwörter*

My/your/his/her/its/our/their sind besitzanzeigende Fürwörter und werden vor Hauptwörtern verwendet, um aufzuzeigen, wem etwas gehört (z. B. Shall I give you Sandra's fax number? = Shall I give you her fax number?).

Modale Hilfsverben (→ Unit 1 und 6)

Die modalen Hilfsverben *can/could/dare/may/might/must/need/ ought to/shall/should/will/would* werden verwendet, um von Ereignissen zu reden, die zum Beispiel (un)nötig, (un)möglich oder (un)wahrscheinlich sind (z. B. You needn't call me back) oder um zum Beispiel (Un-)Fähigkeit, (Un-)Freiwilligkeit oder (Un-)Sicherheit auszudrücken (z. B. Can I help you?).

Fragen (→ Unit 1, 3, 7 und 8)

1 *Fragen mit Fragewörtern*

In Fragen, die mit einem Fragewort wie z. B. *who/where/why/ how (long/much/many)/when/what/which/whose* beginnen, muss das Hilfsverb (do, be, have) oder das modale Hilfsverb (siehe oben) vor dem Subjekt stehen. Die Antworten auf solche Fragen beziehen sich direkt auf die Fragewörter (z. B. Where are you phoning from? – From a call box at Piccadilly Circus).

2 *Fragen mit Yes-/No-Antworten*

In Fragen, auf die mit *"yes"* oder *"no"* geantwortet wird, muss das Hilfsverb (do, be, have) oder das modale Hilfsverb (siehe oben) vor dem Subjekt stehen und ist das erste Wort des Satzes (z. B. Has Oliver appointed two more directors? – Yes, he has).

Verhältniswörter (→ Unit 2 und 5)

Verhältniswörter wie zum Beispiel *about/at/between/by/for/from/in/near/of/off/on/over/through/ to/under/until* werden vor Hauptwörter oder Fürwörter gestellt, um diese mit anderen Satzteilen zu verbinden (z. B. The phone book is on the table). Verhältniswörter werden oft bei Zeitangaben (z. B. at 3 o'clock) oder bei Raumangaben gebraucht (z. B. in the corner).

Gegenwartsformen (→ Unit 2 und 10)

1 *Einfache Gegenwartsform*

Die einfache Gegenwartsform gilt für wiederholte oder permanente Handlungen und Situationen (z. B. I write two reports a week / Ian lives in Leeds / Do you work at weekends?).

2 *Verlaufsform der Gegenwart*

Die Verlaufsform der Gegenwart gilt für eine Handlung oder Situation, die im Moment des Denkens oder Sprechens im Verlauf ist (z. B. Ms White is talking on the phone right now / I am putting you through now / Are they dealing with our request?). Sie wird auch benutzt, um Vorhaben in der näheren Zukunft auszudrücken (z. B. What are you doing at the weekend?).

Bestimmungswörter (→ Unit 2)

1 *Artikel*

Der bestimmte Artikel *"the"* steht vor Hauptwörtern, die mit einem Mitlaut oder einem Selbstlaut beginnen (z. B. The meeting will take place next week / The analysis report is ready). Der unbestimmte Artikel *"a"* steht vor Hauptwörtern, die mit einem Mitlaut beginnen (z. B. Could I make a quick phone call?), während *"an"* als unbestimmter Artikel vor Hauptwörtern steht, die mit einem Selbstlaut beginnen (z. B. Ms Norman, an e-mail has just arrived for you) oder mit stummen "h". In bestimmten englischen Ausdrücken unterscheidet sich die Stellung des unbestimmten Artikels vom Deutschen (z. B. in half an hour = in einer halben Stunde).

2 *Hinweisende Fürwörter*

"This" und *"that"* sind hinweisende Fürwörter im Singular, während *"these"* und *"those"* hinweisende Fürwörter im Plural sind. Alle stehen vor Hauptwörtern. Für Personen und Gegenstände, die in der Nähe vom Sprecher stehen, werden *"this"* und *"these"* verwendet (z. B. This line here is free now / I've just received these graphics), während für Personen und Gegenstände, die weiter entfernt vom Sprecher stehen, *"that"* und *"those"* verwendet werden (z. B. Did you see that memo about the telephone conference last week? / Those phones over there are all in use).

Negation (→ Unit 2)

In negativen Sätzen steht das Wort *"not"* nach dem Hilfsverb oder modalen Hilfsverb (z. B. It wasn't a normal Monday morning / I can't reach John at the moment). In einem Satz ohne Hilfsverb oder modales Hilfsverb wird die Negation mit *"not"* und *"do"* gebildet (z. B. I didn't answer my messages).

Befehlsform (→ Unit 3 und 9)

Die Befehlsform wird verwendet, um zum Beispiel Befehle, Instruktionen und Warnungen zu erteilen, um Vorschläge zu machen oder um etwas zu bitten. Das Verb steht in bejahten und verneinten Sätzen in der Nennform (z. B. Put me through to accounts, please / Don't use the office phone for private calls).

Zukunftsformen (→ Unit 3 und 10)

1 *will*

Die Zukunft mit *"will"* wird verwendet, um eine Situation vorauszusagen (z. B. Please answer the phone – it will be Tanson

Holdings) oder wenn eine zukünftige Handlung im Moment des Sprechens entschieden wird (z. B. Could anyone type this letter for me? – OK, I'll do it, Sue!).

2 *be going to*

Die Zukunft mit *"be going to"* wird verwendet, um eine Situation vorauszusagen, die das direkte Resultat der gegenwärtigen Situation ist (z. B. Oh, no! Look at the fax machine! It is going to run out of paper!), oder um von einer zukünftigen Absicht zu sprechen, die schon entschieden ist (z. B. I am going to take a year off and travel around the world).

Einfaches Imperfekt (→ Unit 4 und 10)

Das einfache Imperfekt wird bei abgeschlossenen Ereignissen und Vorfällen oder bei wiederholten Handlungen in der Vergangenheit verwendet (z. B. Joe phoned a colleague yesterday / We held a meeting every six weeks last year / We didn't see the project outlines / When did you write the letter?). Das einfache Imperfekt wird oft zusammen mit bestimmten Zeitausdrücken wie *yesterday, last week* und *in September 1997* verwendet (z. B. I sent you an e-mail yesterday).

Einfaches Perfekt (→ Unit 4 und 10)

Das einfache Perfekt wird verwendet, um von vergangenen Ereignissen und Handlungen zu sprechen, die eine Verbindung mit der Gegenwart haben. Es beschreibt eine Handlung, die in der Vergangenheit begann und bis zum gegenwärtigen Moment andauert (z. B. We have been on the phone for an hour now); oder es beschreibt eine vollendete Handlung, deren Resultat sich auf die Gegenwart auswirkt (z. B. I have lost Ben Challen's phone number = I haven't got it now). Das einfache Perfekt wird oft zusammen mit unbestimmten Zeitausdrücken wie *ever, never, before, yet* und *already* verwendet (z. B. The client has responded to our letter already).

there is/there are (→ Unit 4)

"there + be" (in der entsprechenden Zeitform) deutet an, dass etwas existiert oder nicht existiert, und steht vor dem Subjekt

(z. B. There is a call for you / There have been three trade fairs already this year / There were not any worthwhile suggestions at the meeting / Have there been any calls for me?).

some und any (→ Unit 5)

Die unbestimmten Fürwörter *some* und *any* stehen vor unzählbaren Hauptwörtern und vor Hauptwörtern im Plural, um eine unbestimmte Menge auszudrücken. *Some* wird normalerweise in bejahten Sätzen (z. B. Here's some information regarding the trade fair) und in Fragen verwendet, wenn eine positive Antwort erwartet wird (z. B. Have you got some news for me? – Ah, thank you!). *Any* wird normalerweise in verneinten Sätzen (z. B. We haven't had any feedback yet) und in neutralen Fragen verwendet (z. B. Why can't we find any temporary secretaries?).

Frageanhängsel (→ Unit 6 und 10)

Frageanhängsel werden an das Ende eines Satzes angehängt, um eine Bestätigung oder Zustimmung zu erbitten. Sie werden aus einem Hilfsverb oder einem modalen Hilfsverb und aus einem persönlichen Fürwort gebildet. Ein bejahter Satz hat normalerweise ein verneintes Frageanhängsel, während ein verneinter Satz ein bejahtes Frageanhängsel hat (z. B. His line is still busy, isn't it? / They didn't inform the marketing department, did they?).

Eigenschaftswörter (→ Unit 6)

Eigenschaftswörter werden verwendet, um Hauptwörter näher zu beschreiben, und bleiben unverändert, egal ob das Hauptwort im Singular oder im Plural steht (z. B. An interesting phone call / A few interesting phone calls). Eigenschaftswörter in der *1. Steigerungsform* werden verwendet, um zwei oder mehr Hauptwörter zu vergleichen (z. B. Danford Ltd is an older firm than Britstone Holdings); Eigenschaftswörter in der *2. Steigerungsform* werden verwendet, um ein einziges Hauptwort vor anderen in einer Gruppe auszuzeichnen (z. B. This project is our most successful one yet).

Verlaufsform des Imperfekts (→ Unit 7)

Die Verlaufsform des Imperfekts versprachlicht eine Handlung, die zu einer bestimmten Zeit in der Vergangenheit stattfand (z. B. I was talking on the phone at four o'clock yesterday). Erscheint die Verlaufsform des Imperfekts zusammen mit dem einfachen Imperfekt im gleichen Satz, gilt die Verlaufsform des Imperfekts für eine längere Hintergrundshandlung, die schon im Gang war, während das einfache Imperfekt für eine kürzere, unterbrochene Handlung gilt (z. B. The partners were just discussing the new deal when the phone rang and the client cancelled it).

Indirekte Rede (→ Unit 7)

Die indirekte Rede wird verwendet, um die Worte von einer Drittperson wiederzugeben (z. B. Sarah says: "David is very busy" = Sarah says that David is very busy). Steht das einleitende Zeitwort im Imperfekt, wird die Zeit in der indirekten Rede eine Zeitstufe rückwärts verschoben (z. B. Sarah said: "David is very busy" = Sarah said that David was very busy).

Verlaufsform des Perfekts (→ Unit 8)

Die Verlaufsform des Perfekts wird verwendet, um von vergangenen Handlungen zu sprechen, die eine Verbindung mit der Gegenwart haben. Sie gilt für eine Handlung, die in der Vergangenheit begann und bis zum gegenwärtigen Moment bzw. bis vor kurzem andauerte (z. B. I have been waiting for twenty minutes now / I've been living here since January. How long have you been learning English?).

Umstandswörter (→ Unit 8)

Umstandswörter beschreiben Zeitwörter und Eigenschaftswörter näher; sie drücken aus, *wie* eine Handlung stattfindet (z. B. Could I use your phone quickly, Sandra?). Die meisten Umstandswörter werden mit *-ly* gebildet, das an das Eigenschaftswort angehängt wird. Es gibt auch Ausnahmefälle, in denen das Eigenschaftswort unverändert bleibt und mit dem Umstandswort identisch ist (z. B. You've been working too hard,

Sue!). Eine weitere Ausnahme ist das Umstandswort *well* – das entsprechende Eigenschaftswort heißt *good*.

would (→ Unit 9)

would kann gebraucht werden, um *hätten (gern)*, *möchten*, *wären* und *würden (gern)* zu übersetzen (z. B. Wären Sie bereit … = Would you be prepared … / Ich möchte lieber … = I would rather …).

Passiv (→ Unit 9)

Die Passivform wird verwendet, um eine Handlung zu beschreiben, deren „Täter" unbekannt ist, oder wenn es uninteressant ist, den „Täter" zu kennen. Das Passiv wird aus dem Zeitwort *be* (in der entsprechenden Zeitform) und mit dem Partizip Perfekt des Zeitwortes gebildet (z. B. The AGM <u>was held</u> in Bournemouth last year / Your call can't <u>be put</u> through).

Schlüssel zu den Übungen

Unit 1

Übung 1

1. I / you
2. you / her
3. my (his/her/our/their)
4. they
5. his
6. you (I/he/she/they) / me (you/him/her/us/them)
7. her (my) / her (me/us) / it / its
8. my (our) / him / his
9. your / me
10. I (she/he/we/they) / my (her/his/our/their)

Übung 2

1. = d	2. = f	3. = g	4. = a	5. = i
6. = e	7. = b	8. = h	9. = j	10. = c

Übung 3

(Musterantwort)

Hi, Andy. I tried to call you this morning, but couldn't get through. I'm off now, so could you let me have some information about next month's trade exhibition? I need to know the date and the place, if possible by this evening. Send me a fax or leave a message on my answering machine.

Thanks and regards,

Elizabeth

Übung 4

1. Good morning, Anderton Limited. How can (may) I help you?
2. I'm sorry, his line's engaged. – How long do you want to wait?
3. My fax number is 478 6554. – What is (What's) yours?
4. How much time do (will/would) you need to write the report?
5. The project meeting is next month. Where shall (can) we hold it?

Test

my/His/me/could/she/me/could/Your/me/should

Unit 2

<u>Übung 1</u>
1. = to 2. = on (at) 3. = of 4. = at (in) 5. = in 6. = for 7. = by (on) 8. = from (for) 9. = through 10. = until (till/at)

<u>Übung 2</u>
1. is talking 2. dictates 3. am connecting 4. doesn't come in 5. aren't bringing 6. never speak 7. are you holding 8. does Annie start 9. Are you sending 10. Do they ever answer

<u>Übung 3</u>
(Musterantwort)
Angela – a Ms Marshall rang while you were away. She wants to discuss proposals for a new project and would like you to phone her back as soon as possible.

Tony

<u>Übung 4</u>
1. a 2. Those (The) 3. This (The) 4. a / the (a/that) 5. this (that/a) 6. these 7. This / the 8. this 9. an 10. These (Those)

<u>Test</u>
wasn't/wasn't/didn't sit/didn't answer/weren't/wasn't/couldn't/mightn't/didn't laugh/didn't say/wouldn't

Unit 3

<u>Übung 1</u>
1. Answer 2. Put 3. go 4. Send 5. Hold 6. worry 7. use 8. ring (call) 9. shout 10. call

<u>Übung 2</u>
1. will ('ll) 2. are going to 3. will ('ll) 4. will ('ll) 5. am going to 6. is going to 7. will ('ll) 8. is going to 9. will ('ll) 10. am going to

Übung 3
(Musterantwort)
Good morning, Mr Smithson, it's Jackie Flint from Ergo Limited. I'm phoning to arrange a lunch meeting for next week. I suggest Thursday at one o'clock at "Valentino's" – what do you think? Call me back to confirm it. Thanks, bye.

Übung 4
1. How 2. When 3. Where 4. Which 5. How long 6. What 7. How many 8. Why 9. Who 10. How much

Test
information/confidential/accompany/Certainly/outline

Unit 4

Übung 1
1. was 2. phoned / were 3. handled 4. wrote 5. ran 6. did / send 7. Did / speak 8. did / answer 9. did / see 10. were

Übung 2
1. is 2. are (will be) 3. were 4. was 5. is 6. were 7. Is 8. Was

Übung 3
Fehlende Wörter:
holding discuss department memo Personnel staff contracts budgeting responsible Advertising

Übung 4
1. has booked 2. have / received 3. has forgotten 4. have lost 5. have / outlined 6. has / given 7. Have / returned 8. Has / told 9. have / been 10. has / done

Test
briefly/pertaining/strategy/follows/dealing/implementation/concept/department/handle/charge/recruitment/arrangements/meeting/outcome/successful

Übung 1
1. some **2.** any **3.** any (some) **4.** some (any)
5. some (any) **6.** any **7.** some (any) **8.** any (some)

Übung 2
1. quarter past two in the afternoon
2. half past seven in the morning
3. eleven o'clock at night (in the evening)
4. quarter to ten in the morning
5. six o'clock in the evening (in the afternoon)
6. ten past twelve in the afternoon
7. twenty-five past six in the morning
8. twenty-five to four in the afternoon
9. ten to eleven in the morning
10. one minute to (midnight) twelve at night (in the evening)

Übung 3
(Musterantwort)
Dear Mrs Hurley,

I hope you are well. I'd like to meet you to discuss project deadlines, and suggest you come to my office in two weeks' time, on Friday 13th September at ten thirty a.m. The main points to be discussed are departmental deadlines and exhibition deadlines.

Please let me know if the above date and time are convenient.

Thank you and kind regards,

Sarah Walker

Übung 4
1. = b) **2.** = a) **3.** = b) **4.** = c) **5.** = a)

Test
Wolfgang thought that "half seven" meant "halb sieben", so he arrived at six thirty and had to wait for an hour (half seven = half past seven).

Unit 6

Übung 1

1. What can I do for you?
2. I would like to speak to Mrs Waterson
3. Could you spell that, please?
4. I must (have to) speak to Sarah Ward urgently.
5. Shall I write that down?

Übung 2

1. isn't it 2. wouldn't you 3. mustn't we 4. doesn't it 5. haven't they 6. can it 7. are you 8. will they 9. do they 10. did she

Übung 3

(Musterantwort)

Dear Maggie,

Here are my details for the trip to the States:

I need a flight leaving Hamburg on Monday 14th March and arriving in New York on the same day. I'll be staying in New York until the Friday, so please book four nights' accommodation at a hotel and the return flight for Friday 18th March, New York to Hamburg.

Thanks a lot,

Mike

Übung 4

1. most successful 2. best 3. oldest / most 4. most interesting 5. farthest (furthest) 6. the fastest 7. earliest 8. most significant 9. most efficient 10. worst

Test

life/favour/missed/could/sure/handout/appreciate/bell

Unit 7

Übung 1

1. was still typing 2. were discussing 3. was designing / was writing 4. were talking 5. were not functioning 6. was not writing up 7. Were / drawing up 8. Was / briefing 9. were / talking to 10. was / doing / was entertaining

Übung 2
1. Is Jill Norman holding the first meeting in two weeks' time?
2. Do they exhibit their new products at every trade fair?
3. Will Rosemary complete the task in time?
4. Are we going to draw up the contracts next week?
5. Did Messrs Trowbridge and Sons deal with the marketing?
6. Was his phone engaged the whole morning?
7. Has Oliver appointed two more directors?
8. Were they designing new layouts all day yesterday?
9. Can you outline the regulations to the new members of staff, Bill?
10. Isn't there enough background information?

Übung 3
1. richtig 2. falsch 3. falsch 4. falsch 5. richtig
6. falsch 7. falsch 8. richtig

Übung 4
1. David Saunders was extremely busy.
2. Georgina and Rick couldn't make it to the meeting.
3. they weren't bringing out a new edition yet.
4. Margaret didn't have time to attend all the meetings.
5. she would call them back as soon as possible.
6. Simon Kirk and James Walker were going to give a presentation.
7. my assistant booked my flights for me.
8. Mr Charlton could give him (her) a ring when he had time.

Test
1. connecting 2. apologise 3. engaged 4. ringing (telephoning/phoning) 5. annual 6. in full swing
7. schedule 8. appoint

Unit 8

Übung 1
1. = d 2. = c 3. = a 4. = e 5. = b

Übung 2
1. quickly 2. personally 3. possibly 4. correctly
5. hard 6. loudly 7. well 8. officially
9. immediately 10. promptly

Übung 3
(Musterantwort)
Dear Sally,

Please set up a telephone conference with the press officers of all four subsidiary companies on Tuesday, 19th January from two to four o'clock in the afternoon.

Thanks a lot,

Tim Herbert

Übung 4
1. 4.25 p.m. 2. 8 a.m. 3. 7.10 p.m. 4. 11.35 a.m.
5. 3.30 p.m. 6. 10.40 p.m. 7. 9.15 a.m. 8. 8 p.m.
9. 2.05 p.m. 10. 2.45 a.m.

Test
how/What/how many/Who/Where/how long/Why/When

Unit 9

Übung 1
1. Would you be prepared to speak to our partners?
2. Would you spell that please?
3. I would rather go to the office first.
4. We would like some information about the next meeting.
5. I would like to speak to Mr Edwards on business.
6. It would be a good idea to discuss your proposals with us.
7. Would you like to leave a message?
8. I would like his extension number.

Übung 2
1. was 2. be 3. been 4. are (were) 5. been 6. are
7. were 8. was 9. be 10. was

Übung 3
Antwort: C

Übung 4
1. be 2. get 3. Try (Call/Phone/Ring) 4. Tell
5. Deal 6. book 7. Inform (Tell) 8. ignore
9. set up (arrange) 10. Make (Take)

Test
1. = a) 2. = c) 3. = c) 4. = a) 5. = b)

Unit 10

Übung 1
1. = b) 2. = c) 3. = a) 4. = c)

Übung 2
1. has / analysed 2. did / have 3. sent 4. has responded
5. Did / write up 6. Have / met 7. has / been (did / go)
8. did / complete

Übung 3
(Musterantwort)
Good morning, Mr/Mrs .... How are you?

Well, we have finally completed the project and I just wanted to thank you very much for all your efforts. I congratulate you on the success you have achieved for yourself and for the company as a whole. I can tell you that the product has been very well received and that we hope to win quite a few new important clients. Once again, thank you and I hope to see you soon.

Goodbye for now!

Übung 4
1. = g 2. = j 3. = d 4. = i 5. = f 6. = h 7. = e
8. = c 9. = b 10. = a

Schlußtest
A/my (some)/most embarrassing/worst/of/sitting/for/How/greeted/began/in/through (about/around)/wildly/some/can/that/waiting/them/any

Wörterverzeichnis

(geordnet nach Unit 1–10)

A

abbreviation	Abkürzung U 3
accommodation	Unterkunft U 6
accompanied	begleitet U 9
accompany	begleiten U 2
according to	zufolge; laut U 7
according to schedule	planmäßig U 7
accordingly	(dem)entsprechend U 5
accountant	Buchhalter(in *f*) U 7
Accounts	Buchhaltung U 3, U 6
achieve	erreichen U 9
acquisition	Anschaffung U 6
act	handeln; unternehmen U 4
actually	eigentlich U 3, U 6
Administration	Verwaltung U 6
administrative assistant	Verwaltungsassistent(in *f*) U 7
advantage	Vorteil U 3
advertised	ausgeschrieben U 5
advertisement	Werbung; Reklame; Anzeige U 8
Advertising	Werbeabteilung U 6
advice	Rat(schlag) U 5
a few minutes ago	vor ein paar Minuten U 4
affair	Angelegenheit U 6
afford	sich leisten U 3
after all	schließlich U 7
agenda	Tagesordnung U 6
AGM (= Annual General Meeting)	Jahreshauptversammlung U 9
ahead	um … voraus U 8
a.m. (ante meridiem)	Vormittag U 5
ambulance	Krankenwagen U 3
amusing	lustig U 2
angle	Standpunkt U 9
annual	jährlich U 6
anticipated	vorausgesehen; erwartet U 10
anticlimax	Enttäuschung U 9
apologise	sich entschuldigen U 7
apology	Entschuldigung U 9
appendix (*pl.* appendices)	Anhang U 8
apply	gelten U 5
appoint	einstellen U 7, U 8
appointed	verabredet; festgelegt U 5
appointment	Termin; Verabredung U 2, U 4
appreciate	schätzen U 6

I'd appreciate that.	Das wäre sehr nett von Ihnen. U 6
approximately (approx.)	ungefähr U 7, U 8
area code	Gebietsvorwahlnummer U 6
arrangement	Abmachung; Verabredung U 4
as always	wie immer U 4
as follows	wie folgt U 4
as soon as	so bald (wie) U 2
as soon as possible	so bald wie möglich U 3
as usual	wie üblich; wie gewöhnlich U 2, U 3
assume	annehmen U 2
at all	irgendwie U 2
at last	endlich U 8
at length	lange; ausführlich U 4
at long last	schließlich und endlich U 10
at my expense	auf meine Kosten U 10
at present	augenblicklich; zurzeit; im Moment; im Augenblick U 1, U 3
at the moment	zurzeit; augenblicklich U 5
at times	manchmal U 8
attach	beiheften U 8
attend (a meeting)	an (einem Treffen) teilnehmen; besuchen U 7
auction	Versteigerung U 10
audit	prüfen U 6
available	frei; verfügbar; *auch:* erhältlich U 3
award	Preis; Auszeichnung U 9
aware	bewusst U 10
awkward	ungünstig U 9

B

base on sth.	basieren auf etwas U 4
bear up	sich halten U 7
be cut off	unterbrochen werden U 9
be due to do sth.	etwas tun sollen U 5
behind	um … hinterher U 8
be in charge	verantwortlich sein U 3
be lucky	Glück haben U 5
be off	gehen U 1, U 4
be pressed for time	unter Termindruck stehen U 9
be reconciled to sth.	sich mit etwas versöhnen U 3
be rushed off one's feet	dauernd auf Trab sein U 4
be the order of the day	auf der Tagesordnung stehen U 5
be underway	in Gang sein U 7
between	zwischen U 5
bid	Versuch U 6
billion	Milliarde U 7
body	Organ U 4
book	buchen; reservieren U 4
born	geboren U 9
borrow	borgen; ausleihen U 2
bother	Ärger U 6
brief	instruieren U 7

briefing	Instruktionen; Anweisungen **U 4**
briefly	kurz **U 4**
bring out	herausbringen **U 2**
budgeting	Budget **U 4**
built-in (*or:* **inbuilt**)	eingebaut **U 1**
business meeting	Geschäftssitzung **U 1**
busy	beschäftigt **U 3**
by the sound of it	offensichtlich **U 7**
by the way	übrigens **U 3**
bye for now	bis bald **U 3**

C

call back later	später zurückrufen **U 1**
call box	Telefonzelle **U 3**
campaigne	Kampagne; Aktion **U 10**
cancel	absagen; fallen lassen **U 1**
cancel	rückgängig machen; streichen **U 7**
case	Fall **U 4**
casual	informell **U 4**
casual	zwanglos; ungezwungen **U 5**
catch	erwischen **U 4, U 5**
celebrate	feiern **U 8**
chat	Plauderei; Schwatz **U 5**
Christmas	Weihnachten **U 2**
circulation	Auflage **U 9**
clearly	klar; deutlich **U 2**
coast guard	Küstenwache **U 3**
collate	zusammentragen **U 8**
colleague	Arbeitskolleg(in *f*) **U 4**
collect call (*US*)	R-Gespräch **U 8**
come across sth.	treffen auf etwas **U 6**
comment	Bemerkung **U 5**
commodity	Ware **U 6**
compared to	verglichen mit **U 7**
complaint	Beschwerde; Klage **U 4, U 7**
compromise	einen Kompromiss schließen **U 5**
concept	Idee; Konzept **U 4**
conclude	abschließen **U 9**
concrete	konkret **U 3**
conduct	führen **U 4**
conference	Konferenz **U 2**
confidential	vertraulich **U 3, U 7**
confirmation	Bestätigung **U 1, U 6**
connect	verbinden **U 1**
I'm connecting you now.	Ich verbinde Sie jetzt. **U 1**
consecutively	nacheinander; hintereinander **U 5**
consensus	Übereinstimmung **U 9**
considering	wenn man bedenkt **U 8**
continuous	ununterbrochen **U 1**
contracting	Verträge abschließen **U 6**
convenient	günstig; passend **U 9**

cope with sth.	zurechtkommen mit etwas U 7
corner	Ecke U 10
corporation	(Handels-)Gesellschaft U 10
corridor	Gang U 10
Could he call me back?	Könnte er mich zurückrufen? U 2
Could I leave a message?	Könnte ich eine Nachricht hinterlassen? U 2
Could I speak to …?	Könnte ich mit … sprechen? U 1
council	Gemeinde U 4
counselling	Beratung U 5
count	zählen U 8
counterpart	Gegenstück; *hier:* Gesprächspartner(in *f*) U 6
country code	Landesvorwahlnummer U 6
courtesy	Höflichkeit U 5
courteously	höflich U 7
crash	abstürzen U 3
create	(er)schaffen U 3
cross	überqueren U 10
crossroads	Straßenkreuzung U 10
Customer Service(s)	Kundendienstabteilung U 6
cut things/it fine	knapp sein/werden U 8

D

dawn on sb.	jdm. dämmern U 10
deadline	(letzter) Termin U 5
deal	Geschäft; Handel U 7
debrief sb.	den Einsatz (anschließend) besprechen mit jdm. U 9
decade	Jahrzehnt U 1
decide	sich entscheiden U 2
deliver	liefern U 9
department	Abteilung U 6
depend on sth.	abhängen von etwas U 2
deputy manager	stellvertretender Betriebsleiter(in *f*) U 3
derivation	Ableitung U 1
detail	Einzelheit; Detail U 4
determine	bestimmen U 6
dial	(eine Nummer) wählen U 2
dialling tone	Amtszeichen U 1, U 10
dictate	diktieren U 2
die-hard	Ewiggestrige(r) U 3
differ	sich unterscheiden U 8
digit	Ziffer; Bestandteil U 6
direct line	Durchwahlnummer U 3
directory enquiries	Auskunft U 3
disadvantage	Nachteil U 3
discuss	besprechen U 3
dissatisfied	unzufrieden U 7
distraught	verzweifelt; außer sich U 7
disturbed	gestört U 1
Do you still want to hold?	Wollen Sie noch warten? U 1
Done!	Abgemacht! U 5

draft form	Entwurf **U 6**
draw up a contract	einen Vertrag aufsetzen **U 6**
draw up	aufsetzen; aufstellen **U 4**
drop	fallen lassen **U 3**
due	fällig **U 7**

E

edition	Auflage **U 7**
efficient	leistungsfähig **U 6**
embarrassed	verlegen **U 1**
embarrassing	peinlich **U 10**
emergency	Notfall **U 3**
employ	anstellen; beschäftigen **U 6**
employee	Angestellte(r) **U 6**
enable	ermöglichen **U 8**
engaged	besetzt; *auch:* verlobt **U 1**
enhance	erhöhen **U 7**
enough	genug; genügend **U 2**
enquire / inquire about sth.	sich nach etwas erkundigen **U 2, U 5**
entail	erforderlich machen; darin bestehen **U 10**
entertain	unterhalten **U 7**
equipment	Ausrüstung **U 7**
era	Epoche **U 10**
estimate	Kostenvoranschlag; Schätzung **U 8**
estimated time of arrival	geschätzte Ankunft **U 5**
even	sogar; selbst **U 2**
evening	Abend **U 5**
eventually	schließlich **U 6**
ever	je(mals) **U 6**
exhibit	ausstellen **U 7**
expand	erweitern; expandieren **U 3**
expenditure	Ausgaben **U 8**
exposure	Publicity **U 9**
express	ausdrücken **U 10**
extension number	Durchwahlnummer **U 6**

F

facility	Einrichtung **U 4**
failure	Misserfolg **U 4**
faint	entfernt **U 8**
far ahead	(weit) voraus **U 3**
fault reporting	Störungsdienst **U 3**
faulty	defekt **U 8**
favour	Gefallen **U 6**
feature	(einen Beitrag) bringen **U 2**
feedback	Feedback; Reaktion **U 5**
fetch	(ein)bringen **U 10**
figure	Zahl; Statistik **U 6, U 7**
file	Ordner **U 3**
filofax	eine Art Agendabuch / Telefonverzeichnis **U 1**
finally	endlich **U 10**

Finance	Finanzabteilung **U 6**
fire away	losschießen **U 9**
firm	Firma **U 4**
fix a date	einen Termin festlegen **U 5**
floor	Stockwerk **U 10**
free of charge	kostenlos; gratis **U 2**
freightline(s)	Frachtfirma **U 10**
further	weiter **U 4**
G	
gambling	Spielen; Wetten **U 5**
generate	erzeugen; entwickeln **U 1**
get a crossed line	jdn. in der Leitung haben **U 8**
get a word in edgeways	überhaupt zu Wort kommen **U 1**
get hitched	heiraten **U 1**
get married	heiraten **U 1**
get through	durchkommen **U 8**
giant	Riese; Gigant **U 10**
give as good as you get	es jdm. mit gleicher Münze heimzahlen **U 10**
give sb. a bell	jdn. anrufen **U 6**
give sb. your apologies	sich bei jdm. entschuldigen lassen **U 1**
glad	froh **U 5**
Go ahead.	Machen Sie (ruhig) weiter. **U 2**
golden rule	goldene Regel **U 7**
government	Regierung **U 4**
graphics	Zeichnungen **U 2**
Greenwich Mean (*or:* Meridian) Time	Greenwicher Zeit; Westeuropäische Zeit **U 7**
greeting	Begrüßung **U 3, U 5**
guide	Führer **U 4**
H	
hamlet	Weiler; kleines Dorf **U 10**
handle	erledigen; bearbeiten **U 4**
happen	geschehen; passieren **U 5**
hardly	kaum **U 8**
have sth. in common	etwas miteinander gemein haben **U 8**
heading	Stichwort; Rubrik **U 4**
helpline	telefonische Seelsorge **U 5**
Hey presto!	Hokuspokus! **U 8**
hi-tech (= high technology)	hochtechnologisch **U 8**
hilarious	komisch; lustig **U 8**
His line's engaged.	Seine Leitung ist besetzt. **U 1**
hold	veranstalten **U 1**
I'll hold, please.	Ich warte bitte. **U 1**
hold the line	am Apparat bleiben **U 1**
holdings	Gutsbesitz **U 2**
home number	Privatnummer **U 6**
hotel manager	Hotelleiter(in *f*) **U 2**
How can I help you?	Wie kann ich Ihnen helfen? **U 1**
hurry	sich beeilen **U 1**

I

I'm afraid	es tut mir Leid, aber; leider **U 2, U 5**
I've got all that.	Das habe ich alles notiert. **U 2**
identify	sich ausweisen; identifizieren **U 2**
imagine	sich vorstellen **U 6**
immediately	sofort **U 2, U 3**
immersion	Vertieftsein **U 7**
implement	durchführen; ausführen **U 5**
implementation	Ausführung **U 4**
in advance	im Voraus **U 4**
inaugural	Eröffnungs-; in Wirklichkeit **U 10**
in case	falls **U 9**
incisive	treffend; präzise; *auch:* scharfsinnig **U 6**
increase	Zunahme; Steigerung **U 4**
increasingly	zunehmend **U 8**
indeed	allerdings **U 9**
independent	unabhängig; selbstständig **U 4**
in effect	praktisch **U 8**
inform	informieren **U 5**
(in)formal	(in)formell **U 5**
initial	anfänglich **U 4**
insert	einwerfen **U 10**
instant	sofortig **U 1**
instead of	statt; anstelle von **U 5**
instrument	Gerät **U 10**
interference	Störung **U 8**
invent	erfinden **U 9**
invoice	Rechnung **U 10**

J

join	sich anschließen; beitreten **U 2**
just a little while	nur kurz **U 1**
just one moment	einen Augenblick, bitte **U 1**

K

keep in touch	auf dem Laufenden / in Kontakt bleiben **U 8**
Keep in touch!	Lass wieder einmal von dir hören! **U 8**
keep sth. in mind	etwas im Auge behalten **U 2**

L

latest	neueste(r) **U 4**
Latin	lateinisch **U 1**
laugh	lachen **U 2, U 10**
leave a message	eine Nachricht hinterlassen **U 2**
lend	verleihen **U 6**
let's (= let us do that)	oh ja; gern **U 3**
likewise	ebenso; gleichermaßen **U 3**
I like to	ich möchte; ich hätte gern **U 2**
limited ("Ltd")	GmbH **U 1**
link-up	Verbindung **U 3**
liquidate	auflösen **U 9**

local	lokal; Orts- **U 2**
look for	suchen **U 1**
look forward to doing sth.	sich darauf freuen, etwas zu tun **U 5**
M	
main door	Haupteingang **U 10**
make	schaffen; erreichen **U 1**
make it to the (meeting)	es schaffen, zum (Termin) zu kommen **U 7**
manage	schaffen **U 8**
managing director	leitende(r) Direktor(in *f*); Geschäftsführer(in *f*) **U 1**
manners	Sitten (und Gebräuche) **U 2**
map	(Land-)Karte; Stadtplan **U 3**
Marketing	Marketingabteilung **U 6**
marvellous	wunderbar **U 8**
matter	Angelegenheit **U 9**
meet up	sich treffen **U 3**
member	Mitglied **U 1**
memo (= memorandum)	Mitteilung; Notiz **U 2**
mention	erwähnen **U 7**
message	Nachricht **U 3**
minutes	Protokoll **U 7**
misunderstanding	Missverständnis **U 5**
mobile phone	Handy; Mobiltelefon **U 4**
more than	mehr als **U 9**
mountain, cave rescue	Berg-, Höhlenrettungsdienst **U 3**
multi-participant	mit mehreren Teilnehmern **U 8**
Munich	München **U 5**
Muzak	Berieselungsmusik **U 3**
mystery	Rätsel **U 5**
N	
necessary	nötig **U 7**
nevertheless	trotzdem **U 5**
nightmare	Alptraum **U 7**
noise	Lärm **U 8**
normally	normalerweise **U 6**
numerous	zahlreich **U 10**
O	
observant	aufmerksam **U 10**
occasionally	gelegentlich **U 8**
office clerk	Büroangestellte(r *m*) **U 7**
office number	Büronummer **U 6**
on the whole	im Ganzen gesehen **U 9**
opportunity	Gelegenheit; Möglichkeit **U 3**
out all day	den ganzen Tag abwesend **U 2**
outcome	Ergebnis **U 4**
outline	Umriss **U 4**
outline	umreißen; skizzieren **U 3**

outside	draußen **U 5**
over and done with	fertig und vorbei **U 10**
over	vorbei; zu Ende **U 4**
oversee	beaufsichtigen; überwachen **U 4**
overwhelming(ly)	überwältigend; umwerfend **U 10**

P

pace	auf und ab gehen **U 10**
pace	Tempo **U 4**
paid (for)	bezahlt **U 8**
pamphlet	Broschüre **U 8**
participant	Teilnehmer(in *f*) **U 9**
party line	Gemeinschaftsanschluss **U 8**
I'll pass it on to him.	Ich richte es ihm aus. **U 2**
patent	patentieren lassen **U 9**
patient	geduldig **U 9**
personal assistant	Direktionsassistent(in *f*) **U 2, U 3, U 7**
personnel department	Personalabteilung **U 2**
personnel manager	Personalleiter(in *f*) **U 7**
Personnel	Personal(abteilung) **U 3, U 4, U 6**
pertaining to	betreffend **U 4**
Plc (= **public limited company**)	GmbH **U 5**
Please hold the line.	Bleiben Sie bitte am Apparat. **U 1**
pleasure	Vergnügen **U 3**
p.m. (**post meridiem**)	Nachmittag **U 5**
polite	höflich **U 2**
poor	arm **U 5**
pop round	kurz vorbeikommen; vorbeischauen **U 4**
popular	beliebt **U 8, U 9**
post(al) code (*UK*)	Postleitzahl **U 6**
pour down	in Strömen gießen **U 8**
practically	praktisch **U 1**
practise	üben **U 3**
prank	Streich **U 10**
prefer	vorziehen; bevorzugen **U 3**
prerecord	vorher aufzeichnen **U 10**
present	Geschenk **U 2, U 6**
presentation	Vortrag **U 7**
pressure	Druck **U 7**
presumably	vermutlich **U 9**
pretty	ziemlich **U 5**
printer	Drucker(ei) **U 8**
privatise	privatisieren **U 4**
professional body	Körperschaft **U 4**
prognosis	Voraussage **U 7**
promise	Versprechen **U 9**
promotion	Werbung **U 6**
prompt	schnell; pünktlich **U 8**
pronounced	ausgesprochen **U 4**
properly	korrekt; richtig **U 7**

proposal	Vorschlag **U 3**
provision	Beschaffung **U 6**
prudent	wohl überlegt **U 2**
public limited company	Aktiengesellschaft **U 5**
publication	Publikation; Veröffentlichung **U 2**
Purchasing	Einkauf(sabteilung) **U 2, U 6**
put through sb.	jdn. verbinden **U 1**
Shall I put you through?	Soll ich Sie verbinden? **U 1**

Q

questionnaire	Fragebogen **U 6**
quite	ganz; *auch:* ziemlich; genau **U 3, U 7**

R

race ahead	mit Riesenschritten vorangehen **U 10**
rage	Wut **U 10**
range from … (through …) to …	von … (über …) bis … reichen **U 5**
rather than	eher als **U 5, U 6**
ready	fertig; bereit **U 5**
realistic	realistisch **U 5**
reason	Grund **U 9**
receive	empfangen; erhalten **U 1, U 4, U 8**
receiver	Empfänger(in *f*) **U 1**
receiver	Hörer **U 10**
recently	kürzlich; vor kurzem **U 3, U 9**
receptionist	Empfangssekretär(in *f*) **U 7**
reckon	meinen; schätzen **U 10**
record	(Tonband-)Aufnahmen machen **U 3**
recorded	aufgezeichnet **U 3**
recover	erholen **U 10**
recruitment	Einstellung **U 4**
refer	weiterleiten **U 4**
reflect	widerspiegeln **U 6**
regarding	betreffend; über **U 5**
regards	Grüße **U 7**
regulation	Vorschrift **U 7**
release	veröffentlichen **U 7**
release	entlassen **U 9**
relevant	zuständig **U 2**
rename	umbenennen **U 9**
replace (the receiver)	(den Hörer) auflegen **U 10**
replace	ersetzen **U 1, U 10**
reply	erwidern **U 5**
request	bitten; ersuchen **U 7**
requirement	Bedürfnis **U 6**
resist	sich widersetzen **U 3**
resounding	gewaltig; durchschlagend **U 10**
respective	jeweilig **U 4**
rest assured	seien Sie versichert **U 6**
retain	(bei)behalten **U 7, U 9**

return a call	zurückrufen **U 4**
(return)flight	(Hin- und Rück-)Flug **U 6**
reverse(d) charge call (*UK*)	R-Gespräch **U 8**
review	Rückblick; Überblick **U 9**
right	gut; in Ordnung **U 1**
rudeness	Unverschämtheit; Grobheit **U 10**
run out	ablaufen; ausgehen; zu Ende gehen **U 3**
run over (a deadline)	(einen Termin) überziehen **U 7**

S

Sales	Verkaufsabteilung **U 6**
sales director/manager	Verkaufsleiter(in *f*) **U 7**
save	sparen **U 6**
Scottish	schottisch **U 9**
secretary	(Betriebs-)Sekretär(in *f*) **U 7**
separate	einzelne(r) **U 6**
serious	ernst **U 10**
service	Dienst; Dienstleistung **U 3**
set up	vereinbaren; arrangieren **U 8**
shame	schade **U 1**
shareholder	Aktionär(in *f*) **U 9**
shout	rufen; schreien; brüllen **U 3**
significance	Wichtigkeit **U 6**
significant	bedeutend; wichtig **U 6**
similar	ähnlich **U 1**
simple	einfach **U 9**
smile	lächeln **U 6**
speak to sb.	mit jdm. sprechen **U 1**
social calling hours	Anrufzeit **U 2**
sometime	irgendwann **U 3**
sort out	klären; *auch:* aussortieren **U 6**
sound	klingen; tönen **U 4**
source	Quelle **U 9**
speaking	am Apparat **U 1**
special	Sonder- **U 2**
spend	(Geld) ausgeben **U 3**
staff	Personal **U 4**
staff meeting	Personalsitzung **U 4**
straight	direkt; gerade **U 1, U 6**
straight ahead	geradeaus **U 10**
strategy	Strategie **U 4**
street directions	Straßenangaben; Wegbeschreibung **U 10**
stunned	sprachlos; fassungslos **U 1, U 6**
subscriber trunk dialling	Selbstwählferndienst **U 3**
subscriber	Teilnehmer(in *f*); Abonnent(in *f*) **U 4, U 7**
subsidiary (company)	Tochtergesellschaft **U 8**
successful	erfolgreich **U 4**
suggestion	Vorschlag **U 3, U 10**
summons	Aufruf; Aufforderung **U 9**
supplement	Beilage **U 2**
suppose	annehmen **U 6**

surprise	Überraschung U 2
survey	Umfrage U 9, U 10
switchboard	Telefonzentrale U 1
sympathy	Mitgefühl; Mitleid U 7

T

take	dauern U 6
take a call	ein Gespräch entgegennehmen U 5
take care of sth.	sich um etwas kümmern U 7
take delivery of sth.	etwas in Empfang nehmen U 8
take on	annehmen U 8
takeover	Übernahme U 5, U 6
task	Aufgabe U 7
telecommunications	Fernmeldewesen U 5
temper	Wut U 10
temporary	vorübergehend; Aushilfs- U 5
tend	neigen; tendieren U 5
That reminds me …	Dabei fällt mir ein … U 6
That's a relief.	Mir fällt ein Stein vom Herzen. U 7
The customer is always right.	*etwa:* Der Kunde ist König. U 7
The line's still busy.	Die Leitung ist noch besetzt. U 1
The Yellow Pages	die Gelben Seiten U 4
thin air	nichts U 3
though	jedoch; obwohl U 2, U 3
through	durch U 5
time difference	Zeitunterschied U 8
tiny	winzig U 10
title	Anrede U 4
to be reconciled to sth.	sich mit etwas versöhnen U 3
tone	Ton U 1
torrent of abuse	Schwall von Beschimpfungen U 10
towards	auf … zu U 6
trade association	Handelsverband U 4
trade fair	Handelsmesse U 5
trade journal	Handelsjournal U 2
trademark	Warenzeichen U 3
traditional	traditionell U 9
transceive	senden und empfangen U 7
transmit	senden U 1
trick	Streich U 10
tucked away	versteckt U 10
turn	abbiegen U 10
turning	Abbiegung U 10
turn out	sich ergeben U 8
two weeks today	heute in zwei Wochen U 5
typist	Schreibkraft U 7

U

unavoidable	unvermeidlich U 9
unexpected	unerwartet U 2
unfortunately	leider U 1

(un)married	(un)verheiratet U 4
unrelated	ohne Beziehung zueinander U 8
urgency	Dringlichkeit U 10
used	gebraucht; angewendet U 4
user	Benutzer(in *f*) U 1
usually	gewöhnlich; normalerweise U 5
V	
value	Wert U 10
variously	verschiedentlich U 4
vary	sich unterscheiden; abweichen U 2
versus	gegen U 5
vice chairman	Vizepräsident(in *f*) U 7
visitor	Besucher U 10
village	Dorf U 10
voice	zum Ausdruck bringen U 7
W	
watchdog	Wachhund; Wächter; Überwachungsbeauftragte(r) U 4
wave about	herumfuchteln U 10
welfare	Fürsorge U 5
well-known	bekannt U 4
whereby	an dem; woran; wonach U 1
whether	ob U 8
whether … or	ob … oder U 2
wind down	zurückschrauben U 9
wonder	sich fragen U 3, U 7
work number	Geschäftsnummer U 6
workmate	Arbeitskollegin U 10
worried	besorgt U 5
worry	sich Sorgen machen; sich Gedanken machen U 3
worthwhile	lohnend U 4
would	würden U 1
Would you like to hold?	Möchten Sie warten? U 1
you may be in for sth.	du kannst dich auf etwas gefasst machen U 2
you're welcome	bitte sehr U 2
Z	
zip code (= Zone Improvement Plan) (*US*)	Postleitzahl U 6

Unsere Empfehlung

Fit für den Job

Kommunikationstrainer Business English: Vorstellungsgespräche

Trainieren Sie gezielt das Jobinterview in 10 Dialogszenen mit den wichtigsten Fragen des Bewerbers und des Interviewers.

Audio-CD mit Begleitheft (32 Seiten)
ISBN 3-468-21502-9

Kommunikationstrainer Business English: Telefonieren

Trainieren Sie gezielt das Telefonieren mit Englisch sprechenden Geschäftspartnern in 10 Telefondialogen.

Audio-CD mit Begleitheft (32 Seiten)
ISBN 3-468-21504-5

Kommunikationstrainer Business English: Meetings

Gezieltes Sprachtraining für geschäftliche Besprechungen in 10 Dialogszenen.

Audio-CD mit Begleitheft (32 Seiten)
ISBN 3-468-21506-1

Übungen zur Vertiefung der gängigen Sprachmuster für britisches und amerikanisches Englisch. Hörtexte und Business-Wortschatz mit der deutschen Übersetzung im Begleitheft.

www.langenscheidt.de
kundenservice@langenscheidt.de

Langenscheidt Verlag
Postfach 40 11 20 · 80711 München
Tel. 0 89/360 96-0 · Fax 0 89/360 96-222

Langenscheidt
...weil Sprachen verbinden

Unsere Empfehlung

A book that means business!

Wortschatz Wirtschaftsenglisch

Die klare, übersichtliche Gliederung nach Geschäftssituationen und Themen ermöglicht Ihnen gezieltes und effektives Lernen. Die Lernschwerpunkte sind u.a. Korrespondenz, Telefonieren, Geschäftsreisen, Organisation, Marketing, Internationaler Handel, Finanzen und Bankwesen. Viele aktuelle Beispielsätze vermitteln Ihnen praxisnah rund 4 000 wichtige Grundbegriffe für den aktiven Sprachgebrauch im internationalen Geschäftsleben.

384 Seiten, ISBN 3-468-40960-5

Business English Wortschatztraining

Mit zahlreichen Übungen erweitern und aktivieren Sie Ihren Wortschatz mühelos. Amerikanisches und britisches Englisch sowie die neuesten Begriffe und Schlagwörter aus der Wirtschaft werden berücksichtigt. Ideal für Selbstlerner, mit einem ausführlichen Lösungsteil am Ende des Buches. Auch gut geeignet zur Vorbereitung auf Prüfungen in Business English. Die ideale Ergänzung zu „Langenscheidts Wortschatz Wirtschaftsenglisch“.

192 Seiten, ISBN 3-468-40961-3

www.langenscheidt.de
kundenservice@langenscheidt.de

Langenscheidt Verlag
Postfach 40 11 20 · 80711 München
Tel. 0 89/360 96-0 · Fax 0 89/360 96-222

Langenscheidt
...weil Sprachen verbinden